WINDWORD BOOKS FOR YOUNG READERS

Clarence "Rabbit" Myles
(Substitute) James Campbell
(Season 2) Tony Clark

Bobby Lee Herron

Hubert "Bo" Beasley

Emmitt Johnson

Earnest "Fat" Locke

(LHP) T. J. Hawkins
(RHP) Sam "Bam" Brown
(RHP) Jerry Craft

Wayne Fisher

Vernon "Puddin" Higgins
(Season 2) Monroe "Mo" Henderson

(Season 1) Alfred Ray
(Season 2) Emmitt Johnson
(Reserve) "Toothless" Tommy Jones

MY SEASONS ACROSS THE COLOR LINE

Pitching FOR THE Stars

JERRY CRAFT AND KATHLEEN SULLIVAN

Texas Tech University Press

This book is typeset in Melior. The paper used in this book meets the minimum requirements of ANSI/NISO Z39.48-1992 (R1997). ∞

Designed by Kasey McBeath
Cover illustration by Laura Jones Martinez

Library of Congress Cataloging-in-Publication Data
Craft, Jerry, 1937–
    Pitching for the stars : my seasons across the color line / Jerry Craft and Kathleen Sullivan.
        pages cm. — (Windword books for young readers)
    Includes bibliographical references and index.
    Summary: "The story of Jerry Craft, the first white man to play in the West Texas Colored League during the summers of 1959 and 1960 as pitcher for the Wichita Falls/Graham Stars"—Provided by publisher.
    ISBN 978-0-89672-787-8 (hardcover : alk. paper) — ISBN 978-0-89672-788-5 (e-book) 1. Craft, Jerry, 1937—Juvenile literature. 2. Baseball players—Texas, West—Biography—Juvenile literature. 3. Mayors—Texas, West—Biography—Juvenile literature. 4. Negro leagues—Texas, West—Juvenile literature. 5. African American baseball players—Texas, West—History—Juvenile literature. 6. Texas, West--Race relations—Juvenile literature. I. Sullivan, Kathleen, 1969– II. Title.
    GV865.C678C73 2013
    796.357092—dc23
    [B]   2013004974

Manufactured by Thomson-Shore, Dexter, MI (USA); RMA589KJ792, April, 2013
Printed in the United States of America
13 14 15 16 17 18 19 20 21 / 9 8 7 6 5 4 3 2 1

Texas Tech University Press
Box 41037 | Lubbock, Texas 79409-1037 USA
800.832.4042 | ttup@ttu.edu | www.ttupress.org

For my Dad, who always found time to play catch with his son
—JERRY CRAFT

For Johnny, Dad, and Connor, my "Boys of Summer"
—KATHLEEN SULLIVAN

CONTENTS

ILLUSTRATIONS, FOLLOWING P. 46

PREFACE

On a Sunday afternoon in May 1959, I pitched my first game for Mr. Sedberry's team, the Wichita Falls/ Graham Stars. The Stars were an all-black baseball team in the West Texas Colored League, and I was a young white man living in a strictly segregated society. Decades of racial segregation in the South following the Civil War had caused black and white athletes to join separate sports teams and to form separate leagues. The West Texas Colored League formed in 1953 and included the Stars and six other black semi-professional teams that surrounded my small home-town of Jacksboro, located northwest of Fort Worth.

The Stars sometimes played teams outside our league, including independent black, white, Hispanic, and military teams. We faced all-white teams from Bowie, Windthorst, and Sheppard Air Force Base at Wichita Falls. Another military base, Fort Wolters in Mineral Wells, had segregated teams at that time. That means they had a team of only white play-ers and another whole team of only black players; the Stars played the black team.

In Texas in 1959, especially in small towns like Jacks-boro, black and white people lived in separate neighborhoods, ate at separate restaurants, and attended separate churches and schools. While I was growing up, I watched news stories about the early Civil Rights Movement with interest, particularly when Rosa Parks was arrested in Montgomery, Alabama, on December 1, 1955, for refusing to move to the back of the bus to make room for white riders. Across the nation opinions about segregation were changing, but in my world, black and white people still lived separate lives.

During my time with the West Texas Colored League, our teams were loosely organized because we all worked at regular jobs during the week. When we had time off, we traveled in whatever cars were running to games that took place only if enough players arrived by game time. Sure, we kept our own scorecards, but our league standings received no media attention. My memories and those of my surviving teammates, Clarence "Rabbit" Myles and Monroe "Mo" Henderson, form the only record of our time together. The West Texas Colored League never appeared in the two Wichita Falls newspapers, the *Wichita Falls Times Record News* and the *Wichita Falls Times* in the 1950s and 1960s. We were simply too informal of a league to be included on a sports page, and in any case, the papers would never have covered an all-black local team.

While the press ignored us, we were busy facing each team at least twice every summer during 1959 and 1960, usually for one game at home and another game away. Some teams were fun to play, like the Haskell Yellow Dogs. We enjoyed postgame food, refreshments, and fellowship with them at the Yellow Dog Tavern west of Haskell. When we played at home, we scheduled our games on Sunday afternoons at Spudder Park in Wichita Falls and on Wednesday nights at the Graham Public Baseball Field in Graham, a town about sixty miles south of Wichita Falls.

We also played a tournament in Ranger, a small town a little over a hundred miles south of Wichita Falls, during the Juneteenth holiday weekend. Before I joined the Stars, the holiday tournament meant that black teams from across the state entertained their fans with baseball for the long weekend. Fans would travel from near and far to enjoy their time off work and the tournament. When I joined the Stars, we were the first and only team in the West Texas Colored League to integrate, and we enjoyed representing the league at the Ranger Tournament.

When I initially took the mound for the Stars, I had not thrown a baseball to a black person since my sandlot days in my hometown. Our childhood games had been integrated, involving all the children in town. My white grade-school friends and I never questioned why we played baseball with black children but did not go to their schools or even drink from the same water fountains.

The integration of the Stars is more meaningful to me now than in 1959. Back then, I was just happy to play baseball. Mr. Carl Sedberry, Jr., the Stars' manager, simply invited me to play because the team needed good pitching to win. Pitching was hard to find in West Texas, and I was a very good, experienced pitcher who was available, though I was white.

This is the story of my time with the Stars.

—JERRY CRAFT

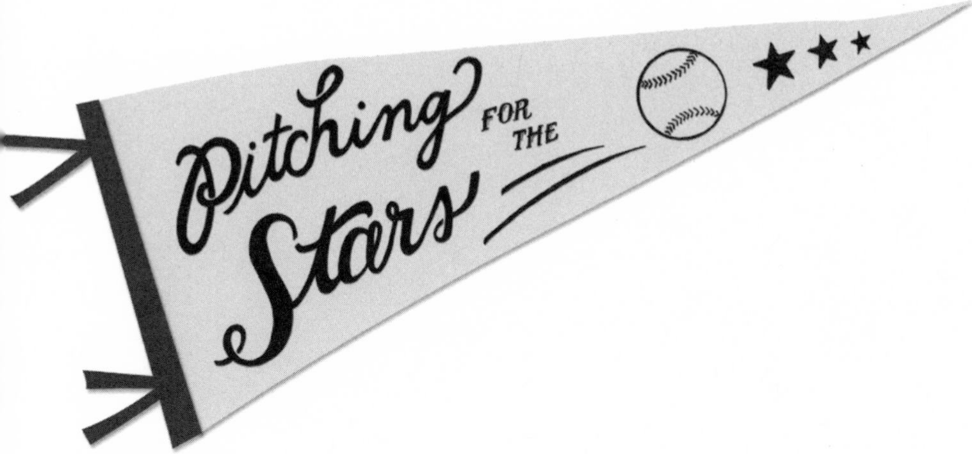
Pitching
FOR THE
Stars

CHAPTER ONE
AN INTERESTING EXPERIMENT

My journey with the Stars began in May 1959, the same day I returned home to Jacksboro, Texas, after completing my fourth year of college at Texas Technological College (now Texas Tech University). I had few plans for the summer except working on my father's ranch and visiting with friends. I was twenty-two years old, a six-foot-two-inch, 185-pound West Texas ranch boy with green eyes and short, wavy, dark brown hair. I had an easygoing personality, but I was always a little self-conscious of the irregularly shaped pupil of my left eye, a result of a childhood accident.

When I was nine years old, I received my first pocketknife for Christmas, the same kind of knife my hero Red Ryder used during the twenty-five-cent Saturday afternoon matinees I saw at the Jack and Mecca Theatres in Jacksboro. I watched in awe as Red threw his knife into a bale of cotton, which must have impressed the outlaw standing next to it because he took his hand away from his holster and retreated. I decided to practice the same move with my own knife.

We did not have any cotton at my house, so I found a bale of hay, propped it against a tree, and threw my knife. It hit the tree, bounced back, and lodged in my left eye. I went inside, where my mother was concentrating on her Christmas present, a Singer sewing machine. Her back was to me when I told her, "Mom, I have a knife stuck in my eye!"

"Um-humm," she replied as she continued sewing.

"Mom, I really do!" I cried.

She turned around, stood up, and fell on the floor. She had fainted at the sight of my eye! The doctors did their best, taping my head tightly to close my eye. When it healed, they wanted me to wear glasses, but my father J. D. would not allow it.

"I want my son to be a very good athlete," he told them. "He can't wear glasses. He will have to adjust."

I did. As a ten-year-old pitcher on the sandlot in Jacksboro, I modified my stretch so that I could check the runner on first base. I am a right-handed pitcher, meaning I would normally use my left eye to watch the runner on first. After the accident, I couldn't see first base as easily with my left eye, so I had to turn my head and use my right eye to watch the runner there.

My eyesight also changed other aspects of my game. As a right-handed batter, I learned to turn my head farther to the left so my right eye could catch the rotation of the ball as it flew out of the pitcher's hand. When I fielded, I also turned my head so that I could catch throws from other players and fly balls. I have never considered my eyesight a handicap, though I often think of that foolish afternoon with the villain bale of hay.

On the day I started my summer break from college, I drove up the semicircular front drive to my parent's large, two-story white-brick house on Live Oak Street in Jacksboro. I could see my mother through the screened-in back porch door. Louise "Lou" Craft was then only forty-five years old, a very petite woman at five foot three inches.

As my mother and I waited for my father to return home from Craft Ranch headquarters for dinner, we visited in the kitchen while she cooked my favorite supper, chicken-fried steak with cream gravy, french fries, pinto beans, biscuits, cherry cobbler, and iced tea. Although it was only May, my mother's homegrown tomatoes were on the table as well.

"A man named 'Sedberry' has called a couple of times to talk to you about playing baseball this summer. I don't know any 'Sedberrys.' Do you know any 'Sedberrys'?" she asked.

"No, I don't," I told her.

I wasn't surprised that someone had called about my pitching. I had played semi-professional baseball for Wichita Falls in the Oil Belt League during the previous two summers, so there was a good chance Mr. Sedberry had seen me pitch then. I told her that I would return the call that afternoon, but I didn't have a chance because Mr. Sedberry called again.

As I was helping my mother set the table for supper, the phone rang.

"Is this Mr. Jerry Craft?" a voice asked.

"Yes sir," I replied. My mother had raised me to be a southern gentleman, so I added "sir" to any "yes" or "no" question from an elder.

"Are you playing any summer ball right now?"

"No sir," I said as I was balancing silverware and plates, the phone cord stretched across the table.

"Well, we really want you to play for our team. I'm Mr. Sedberry, the manager."

I stopped what I was doing to listen more carefully. "Who's your team?"

"The Wichita Falls Stars."

"I never heard of you guys. Are you new?"

"Oh, we've been around a long time. We've got an excellent ball club, but we don't have very good pitching. You're exactly who we need."

I enjoyed hearing compliments about my playing, and a summer job would give me some extra money for school expenses in the fall. "Well, what do you pay?" I asked.

"For a pitcher of your class, $75 a game," he said.

I was really excited. That would be the most money I'd ever been paid for pitching. "How many games a week?" I asked.

"Two games a week," he said. "Wednesday nights and Sunday afternoons."

The total, $150 a week, would be a very large sum of money for a part-time summer job in 1959, so I immediately agreed. "I'd be happy to try out for your team," I said.

"Meet us this Sunday at Spudder Park in Wichita Falls for a game against our old rivals, the Abilene Blues. Play with us and see if you like us, and we'll see if we like you," he said.

"Thank you, Mr. Sedberry. I'll be there."

I hung up the phone and shrugged at my mother. She looked doubtful, so I tried to reassure her.

"It's just a tryout," I told her. "And it's only twice a week. Plus they are going to pay me $75 a game to pitch!"

When my father arrived for supper, our conversation immediately turned to ranch news and the weather. Rainfall, or lack of it, controls how many head of cattle we can sell and how profitable they will be.

When I finally introduced the idea of my playing baseball that summer and explained how much they would pay me, my father responded with mixed emotions.

"I knew you'd probably want to play ball this summer," he said. "I don't understand why they are going to pay you so much money though."

"I don't either, but I want to find out," I said.

Despite his skepticism, my father allowed me to skip my chores on game day. He had work to do, so he couldn't come to see me play.

He wished me luck, and I started the hour-long drive to Wichita Falls alone. I've always been grateful that he did not travel with me. I'm certain he would not have allowed me to walk onto a baseball field with a black team.

Spudder Park was a minor-league baseball park named not for potatoes but after the expression "spudding in an oil well," meaning "drilling a well," back in the early days of oil production. Spudder Park held special memories for me. It was the place where I saw my first major-league game in 1953, the New York Giants versus the Cleveland Indians. When I was attending high school, my friends and I watched Elvis perform at Spudder Park on August 22, 1955. He sang and danced on a temporary stage built between the pitcher's mound and home plate. I had also pitched and won the bi-district championship there during my senior year of high school, defeating Iowa Park 3–0.

Lost in these pleasant memories, I arrived in Wichita Falls early for my Stars tryout, about 1:00 p.m. I got out of my pickup truck and walked toward the main entrance. As I descended the steps that led to the field, I stopped abruptly. The stands held about two hundred black people, and two teams of all-black players were warming up.

"Wrong address," I thought and climbed the stadium steps to return to my truck. I left Spudder Park and drove to two other small ballparks on the west side of town. Both were empty. I had no way to contact Mr. Sedberry, so I returned to Spudder Park to solve this mystery.

No white people were in sight when I pulled back into the parking lot. I then concluded that the black teams must be playing before the white teams. I thought I would wait for the white teams, but I didn't know where to wait for them.

I again got out of the truck and walked slowly back down the stadium steps. The game was less than an hour away from starting, but I still couldn't find my team. Suddenly, a large, well-dressed black man, roughly ten years older than I was, walked toward me, hand outstretched, and said, "Mr. Craft? I'm Mr. Sedberry, Carl Sedberry, Jr."

My mouth dropped open. I shook his hand, and he chuckled and said, "Well, Mr. Craft, you didn't know I was black, did you?"

I slowly shook his hand and carefully considered his appearance. His immaculate blue coat and tie and matching snap-brim hat contrasted sharply with my old Cruise Tire Company uniform. I still wore the same shoes from last summer, so they added to the contrast between me and Mr. Sedberry in his polished dress shoes.

"Mr. Sedberry?" I asked, still shaking his hand. He nodded and smiled silently, steadily returning my gaze. "No sir, I didn't know you were black," I said.

"I didn't mention it because I thought if you knew we were a black baseball club you wouldn't want to play with us. Make any difference?" he asked.

"I'm not sure," I replied, honestly.

"You've played a lot of baseball. Did you ever think about playing for a black baseball team?" he asked.

"No sir, I've never even seen a black baseball team until today. How do you think your team is going to react to me?"

"I don't know. It's going to be an interesting experiment," he said.

"Mr. Sedberry, I don't know if I want to be part of an experiment," I admitted.

"Come with me," he said reassuringly.

We moved down the stadium steps, where I was greeted by Jacksboro's Alfred Ray, the Stars' catcher. I was surprised to see him. I didn't expect to see someone I knew from my childhood, especially under these circumstances.

"Alfred and I scouted you last summer in Wichita Falls, and he suggested that I recruit you," explained Mr. Sedberry.

"It's good to see you again," Alfred said.

"Good to see you too," I told him.

About fifteen minutes later, Mr. Sedberry waved me toward the rest of the team and introduced me as "Mr. Craft." From that day forward, he always called me "Mr. Craft" and I always called him "Mr. Sedberry," although the other players often called him "Carl" or "Junior," and he used their first names as well.

The Stars had assembled around us, and I was received rather coolly, my white face standing out among the black. We were a mismatched bunch, sporting uniforms of various shades and styles. The Stars had all evidently played for other teams in previous seasons and kept their old uniforms or borrowed uniforms for the game.

My teammates eyed me suspiciously while Mr. Sedberry reviewed our game strategy. "Men, you know we've never beaten the Blues, but we will today. They're just arrogant. Now, I think we should start our worst pitcher," Mr. Sedberry said as he slapped a young pitcher on the back. Sam "Bam" Brown was about my age, twenty two, and much skinnier than I was.

"Yes sir," Sam said eagerly, agreeing easily with Mr. Sedberry. I couldn't understand why Mr. Sedberry wanted Sam to start the game. Mr. Sedberry continued explaining his plan.

"Let them get ahead and overconfident, and then we'll put in the big artillery. We'll blow them back to Abilene!" he shouted. The Stars cheered, clapped their hands, and headed back to the field.

I followed Mr. Sedberry to the dugout. "Mr. Sedberry, who's our big artillery?" I asked.

"Why, that's you, baby!" Mr. Sedberry smiled.

A few minutes before the start of the game Mr. Sedberry sent me to the bullpen. "Toothless" Tommy Jones, the bullpen catcher from Breckenridge, Texas, was there, ready to help me warm up. However, he looked old enough to be my grandfather, even older because of his missing teeth.

I waved Mr. Sedberry over. "I don't think he is strong enough to catch me."

"Just throw the ball," Mr. Sedberry replied.

"OK, but I really think I might hurt him," I said.

Mr. Sedberry slowly walked away without another word.

After a few easy pitches, I noticed the old catcher was singing to me. He'd rock back and forth and sing. I got ready to start throwing curves, which all pitchers indicate by flipping their gloved hand over. I said, "I'm going to throw some curves."

"Throw your curves in here, white boy," he replied.

"Yes sir. But you need to watch out for these curves, sir. They're hard to catch." I snapped my wrist downward, which not only produced the spin needed for a curveball but also made the ball drop while it curved.

"Just throw them in here, white boy."

I did, and I hit him on the inside of his right knee. The pitch knocked him off his feet, and he rolled around and hollered for a while.

"Hey, I'm sorry, but I warned you. My curves really drop, just like I told you."

He grunted at me as he got back in his stance. I threw him another curve, and it caught him on the left knee. He finally limped over to Mr. Sedberry. They returned after a few seconds of animated conversation, and Mr. Sedberry approached me.

"Mr. Craft, my catcher says you're hurting him," he said.

"Yes, I'm hurting him. He's too old to play," I said. I stood with my hands on my hips, very sure that my opinion was correct.

"Mr. Craft, do you white boys like playing catcher?" Mr. Sedberry said while we watched the old man try to bend his knees again.

"No sir, we don't," I replied.

"That's right. It's a dangerous and dirty job. Any time I can get a man to play catcher, I'm going to keep him."

This was the first piece of baseball wisdom Mr. Sedberry imparted to me. Old Tommy was doing a job none of us wanted to do, so we needed and valued him. We resumed our warm-ups.

A few pitches later, I let my fastball go. Old Tommy fell backward, but he hung on to it, and then smiled, gums shining in my direction. I returned his smile, and we went to the dugout to sit on the bench together.

The Stars didn't score in the bottom of the first, and the Blues were far ahead, 7–0, in the top of the second inning. With the bases loaded and one out, Mr. Sedberry called time and walked to the mound. He and Sam returned to the dugout.

"All right, Mr. Craft! It's time for you to go get 'em!" he said.

"Mr. Sedberry, it's too late," I said.

After I'd thrown a couple of warm-up pitches to catcher Alfred Ray, I eyed the three runners and agreed to Alfred's signal, firing a fastball to the outside corner. The batter hit a screaming line drive past my left ear. Fortunately, it headed directly toward second baseman Emmitt Johnson, who caught it and stepped on second for an unassisted double play that ended the inning. My new teammates celebrated, and Mr. Sedberry slapped me on the back as I returned to the dugout.

"See, it's starting to work, Mr. Craft," he said.

"Work? Did you see how hard that guy hit the ball?" I asked.

"Patience and faith, Mr. Craft," he said.

The Stars stranded two runners in the bottom half of the second inning. When I returned to the mound for the top half of the third inning, something was very wrong.

The batter, who was the coach's son, stood in the middle of home plate and smiled at me. I had never seen a batter do this, and I didn't know what to do next.

I called time to discuss the batter with my catcher.

"What's he doing?" I asked.

"Waiting for the first pitch, white boy" Alfred replied matter-of-factly. I gathered that the team had nicknamed me "white boy."

"Well, let's try it again," I suggested, thinking that after the Blue had a moment, he'd find the batter's box.

Alfred trotted back to home plate, and the Blue batter again stood in the middle of it.

I could hardly contain my disbelief. I walked him on four straight pitches, protesting the entire time. The next batter, who was the coach's other son, did the same.

I called for Alfred and Mr. Sedberry to join me on the mound again. Mr. Sedberry told me to hit him in the shoulder or leg. "If you don't, every batter is going to do this." Alfred nodded and retreated to behind home plate.

Full of fear and adrenaline, I threw as hard as I could at the batter's left shoulder. Instead of turning away from the ball, he turned into it. The ball hit him right in the heart. Thump! He fell over backward, his legs kicked a couple of times, and his eyes rolled back into his head.

"My God, I've killed this man," I whispered to myself.

The batter lay on the ground, quivering, and the Blues

poured water on him and fanned him with their caps until his eyes rolled back down. "Son, son, is you dead?" the Blues' coach asked.

"No, Daddy, but I almost is," he said.

His boy finally stood up and staggered to first base, crossing back and forth over the foul line as he walked.

I turned toward the plate and glanced at the next batter. To my amazement, he was at least three feet from home plate, his eyes as big as saucers. He was terrified.

Alfred grinned at me from behind his catcher's mask and signaled for a high, inside fastball. I threw slightly inside, and the batter fell to the ground. My next pitch, a curve, broke for a strike. For the third strike, I threw a curve on the outside corner. Again, the batter hit the dirt, and I easily struck out three in a row. Amazingly, I struck out twenty-one Blues that day, and the Stars defeated them for the first time by a score of 7–18!

As I struck out the final batter, the crowd moved their celebration onto the field. The Stars fans swirled around me, and I let them carry me off the mound. I had never played for fans like this before, and I loved it.

"Mr. Craft, you think you'll play another game for us?" Mr. Sedberry shouted above the noise of the crowd.

"Mr. Sedberry," I yelled back, "I'm yours."

CHAPTER TWO
GROWING UP IN JACKSBORO

The Stars and I played baseball for the first time in Wichita Falls in 1959, but baseball and racial segregation have a much longer history in West Texas. In the late nineteenth and early twentieth centuries, small towns like Wichita Falls and neighboring Jacksboro had their own white baseball teams, called town teams. The local team played at Fort Richardson Field, which is now part of Fort Richardson Historical State Park in Jacksboro.

Although no historical marker memorializes the baseball field, the north end of the park is shaped like the lower part of a baseball diamond. The field is near a stone munitions bunker, which was built as part of Fort Richardson and in use from 1866 until 1878. Small vertical slits in the stone allowed the soldiers from the Fourth, Sixth, Tenth, and Eleventh units of the United States Cavalry to fire their weapons from inside the bunker during skirmishes with the Kiowas and Comanches. Battles with Indians raged until 1874, making the Texas soldiers and settlers too busy to play baseball.

In 1881, seven years after the last Indian battle, baseball began to emerge in Jacksboro and the surrounding areas, though the first teams were white. The two original town teams met at the Jack County Courthouse, both calling themselves the Western Pioneers. Two more Jacksboro town teams emerged in 1887, the Jack County Entertainment Independents (J. C. E. I.s) and the True Muffers. Jacksboro had several other town teams from 1888 to the turn of the century, sporting the colorful names Featherlegs, Fat Boys, and Lean Men.

In those days, games between towns were highly organized social as well as athletic events. Entire families would travel by horse and buggy, later by car or pickup truck, for an all-day outing. Families ate picnic lunches while listening to musical performances by the rival town bands at the Fort Richardson Parade Grounds, where Fort Richardson Field was located.

By the 1920s fans traveled to games in the several hundred automobiles that were rumbling through the county. Thanks to faster transportation, attending away games took much less time, especially if the roads were in good shape. Those two lanes of dirt easily turned to mud after the slightest storm. Due to these factors, fans and teams generally limited their travel to a thirty-mile radius.

We owe a great deal of my family's history to the town teams and their games because they gave young people an opportunity to socialize. In fact, my mother met my father on a day he played left field. Sometimes the Jacksboro team wore uniforms, but at this game my father wore jeans, a white dress shirt, and a black bowtie.

Trying to impress her, he stole home with his signature head-first slide, and in doing so, ignited a box of matches in his shirt pocket. He was safe, but the crowd roared with laughter as the catcher used his mitt to beat out the flames.

After the game, my father's friend Ivan waved him over to the stands to introduce him to the lovely young woman he had tried to impress.

"Jay, this is Louise, my sister-in-law. You can call her 'Lou,'" Ivan said.

"Ivan, would you allow me to take this lovely young lady for a ride in my Model T?" Jay asked.

"Yes, of course. If she wants to go," Ivan said.

My father said my mother hesitated for a moment. Finally, she said yes.

They were smitten with each other. After a short, happy courtship of three months, they were married, and my mother moved to Jacksboro.

By the late 1940s, Jacksboro added lights to its field, greatly increasing the number of fans at the games. Crowds from all over the county watched night games at Fort Richardson Field. My family enjoyed those games because my father was slightly more relaxed when he played baseball than at any other time.

My father was a hard worker, whether on the baseball field or at our family's ranch, but he always made time for us at home. When he returned home from the ranch, he'd hit fly balls to me and my younger sister, Linda. He hit baseballs to me and softballs to her. It didn't matter how tired he was.

Over and over we heard his motto: "When you work, work hard. When you play, play hard. Never give up!" He and his generation had survived the Great Depression. No matter what they accumulated in life, they never really felt secure, but on the positive side, they always had a budget and never went deeply into debt.

My sister and I never completely understood my father's

frugality, but we were glad we inherited his athleticism. He was a calf roper in his younger days, and we often went with him to rodeos. Later he traveled the cutting-horse circuit in the 1950s with his horse "Miss Texas," and they became the Reserve Champions of America in 1955. A "reserve champion" means that he actually finished in second place, but it is still a very impressive accomplishment.

Linda and I worked on our family's ranch and had our own horses for rodeos and parades. Linda was a natural athlete. She and I played sandlot baseball together when we were children because there was no organized baseball of any type in Jacksboro until high school. The sandlot was one of the few places in Jacksboro that was not segregated. Kids of all ages just showed up and played, and we never knew who or how many kids would play, black or white.

Our least favorite position was catcher because we had no catcher's mitt, mask, or pads. The catcher stood far behind the batter to avoid injury. For that reason, I didn't want to play catcher.

Fort Richardson Field was just south of Lost Creek, which bordered the black community in Jacksboro. Because the black children lived near the field and creek, they played and swam with us all summer. Baseball games always ended with a swim in the creek's old "Fort Hole," as we called it.

I remember that every child in Jacksboro, black and white, learned to swim in Lost Creek. Regardless of color, we played and swam together in the summers. I didn't consider how my friends from the Lost Creek community felt when they returned to their separate neighborhood in the evenings after our swims or to their separate school in the fall. I was only a child, and I never thought to ask them how they felt about segregation.

Many of my childhood friends are still my friends. Jim Boley, Bobby Murray, Tony Clark, Bob Sikes, Eddie McConnell, and I attended first grade together in 1943. My mother dropped me off early for my first day at the three-story red brick Jacksboro Elementary School. The school at that time enrolled only white students, and on the first day of school I met a new friend, Leonard Jamison.

Leonard lived in the Cooper community, eight miles north of Jacksboro. He wore the unfortunate "country kid" uniform, coveralls. On the playground before school started, a huge kid named Bobby started beating the daylights out of Leonard. I rushed over and tried to push Bobby off Leonard, but Bobby knocked me down and continued hitting him. Determined to save my new friend, I found a good-sized rock and aimed between Bobby's eyes, knocking him out with a terrific pitch.

The principal, Howard Elenburg, caught us both. He then called my mother to take me home early. She was humiliated. I had destroyed my family's good reputation before the bell had rung on my first day of school. Every morning after that first day I dreaded going to school and facing the bully. Then I had an idea.

I arrived on the playground before school started. There I selected a few rocks and stuffed them into my right-hand pants pocket. When the bully Bobby approached me and my buddies, I quickly pulled out a rock and drew back to throw at him. He slowed for a second but continued toward me. I threw one at his knee. He winced and grabbed his knee while I took aim again. This time he scowled and walked away.

If I forgot my rocks, I paid the price. I'm sure the teachers wondered why I always had lumps in my jeans pockets, but they never asked me to empty my pockets. Maybe the teachers were aware of my strategy for dealing with Bobby.

Throwing rocks helped me survive elementary school and develop an accurate pitching arm. Rocks soon became one of my favorite ways to practice baseball, because Jack County had plenty of rocks. I threw them at tin cans when I was at home. Once during a sandlot game when I was ten years old, I threw a rock at a fast-moving jackrabbit crossing Fort Richardson Field and killed it. A couple of the black children on our team asked if they could take it home. Long, lean jackrabbits have tough meat compared to cottontail rabbits, so the rest of us would never have considered eating it.

Next I decided to work on my batting. I took a knife and whittled a broom handle into a flat board to fit a two-handed swing. I would toss the rocks into the air and swing. A rock that cleared the barn was a home run.

I remember that we continued to play sandlot baseball together on integrated teams when I was in elementary school because we needed at least nine players in the field. Whichever nine children were ready to play, black or white, we included them. The black kids didn't own gloves, so when one team was at bat, the other team used the gloves.

My white friends and I had old, flat gloves, handed down from fathers and big brothers, with one leather strip that served as the web between the thumb and forefinger. If the strip broke, and it often did, we used shoestrings to replace it. Under such conditions, there were no one-handed catches. As soon as I caught a ball, I clamped my bare hand over it.

I remember receiving my first, honest-to-goodness, new baseball glove on Christmas Day when I was in fourth grade. To keep the glove soft, I used my father's neat's-foot oil, the same oil he rubbed on his saddles. My new glove had leather strings connecting the fingers and a pocket, which greatly helped my ability to catch and hold a baseball.

On the sandlot we all shared equipment, sparse as it was, especially the few bats we owned. We often used hand-me-down bats that had been tossed aside at the adults' baseball or softball games. Even cracked bats were highly prized because we couldn't afford new ones. We would nail the parts together and tape them heavily with black tape.

Many of my sandlot baseball friends later played football and baseball in my front yard when my family moved to a large house on West Live Oak Street. At my new house, home runs cleared my folks' hedge of cedar trees. After games, we talked about sports, hunting, fishing, and school, but I can't recall any of us, black or white, asking, "How come we go to separate schools?" We just assumed school had always been that way, and we couldn't conceive a world that would be different.

If the black children had opinions about living in a separate part of town or going to a separate school, they never mentioned them to me. In 1959 the city opened a segregated pool, which most of the white children used. After that, only the poor white children who could not afford the price of admission continued to swim at Fort Hole with the black children. I don't recall discussing the segregated pool with my friends. I don't think we could have imagined the new pool, like Jacksboro schools, any differently.

Before integration, Jacksboro had one black school, the Blackshear Colored School, a one-room building that held both the elementary and high school. Located on the banks of Lost Creek, the Blackshear Colored School opened in the fall of 1888 with sixteen students and only one teacher.

Eventually, some young, more progressive members of the white community recognized the injustice of racial segregation in Jacksboro schools. In 1964 the Reverend Ed Gearheart from the local First Presbyterian Church and a group of young men, all of them white, asked to meet with the school board so they could present their case in favor of integration. None of Jacksboro's black citizens appeared at the hearing. They cared for their community's school and didn't want to send their children to a white school. They, like their white neighbors, feared change.

Despite this tense atmosphere, the school board agreed with the group of white leaders that the schools should be integrated and combined. The Blackshear Colored School closed in the spring of 1964, and its teacher, Mrs. Shelton, retired.

After the Jacksboro school system integrated, other formerly all-white areas of our town were soon opened to every citizen. The city pool was formally integrated in the summer of 1965, but I can't remember any black children swimming there until several years later. I don't believe they felt comfortable swimming in the public pool with us, and most of them probably couldn't afford the admission fee.

When my friends and I started high school in 1951, our sandlot baseball games with the black children ended. Instead, we all played sports at the white high school. I was an unusual high school student because I excelled at both athletics and academics. I became a strong student because I loved to read.

I didn't play baseball my first or second spring semesters in high school, 1952 and 1953, because our team didn't have a field. We were building a new field next to Lake Jacksboro, north of town. Tiger Field became a beautiful ballpark, overlooking Lake Jacksboro.

My junior year, 1954, I won the starting job as left fielder, and Tiger Field officially opened. I was a tall, fast outfielder and had a strong throwing arm. I could catch a fly ball and consistently throw the ball with one hop to our catcher.

At Jacksboro High School, our head baseball coach was Wallace "Hogcaller" Myers, so named by the *Fort Worth Star-Telegram* for his piercing screams during his T.C.U. basketball days. He took me aside at the end of the 1954 baseball season and told me that he would probably name me starting pitcher my senior year. I was excited because the pitcher, like the quarterback, was "The Man," someone all my friends would admire.

The spring of 1955 arrived. The grass was green, and baseball season began. I was in great shape from playing football and basketball. Our baseball team was soon a fine defensive club with fair hitting.

We played a standard seven-inning high school game. I became an aggressive base runner, ending the season with a total of twenty-two stolen bases. My sister and her friends attended the games, and they called me "Bubba" when they cheered.

I thoroughly enjoyed playing high school baseball. I believe I was born with a certain amount of pitching talent. I tried to develop my pitching speed by eating large meals, but I never gained the amount of weight I wanted.

I thought lifting weights might help, but my high school didn't have a weight room. Jim Boley and I made weights during our junior year by taking five-gallon buckets, filling them with cement, and sticking the ends of a metal pole in each bucket. They were ugly, but functional, and helped my pitching arm gain strength and endurance.

I finished a very satisfying high-school baseball career with a batting average of .452, an 11–3 won-loss record, a 1.33 ERA (Earned Run Average—the average number of runs scored against a pitcher per game), and only allowed 1.33 walks a game. I was voted MVP of District 9–AA, but I knew that if I wanted to play regularly at the college level, I would need more experience.

I stepped immediately into the semi-pro ranks so that the experience might give me a better chance to play for the Texas Tech Red Raiders in Lubbock, where I had been accepted for the fall semester of college. Our pay as semi-pros, though meager, would not be allowed today under NCAA (National Collegiate Athletic Association) rules. Even though we were "semi-pro," our "pay" depended on the generosity of the crowds, when baseball caps were passed among that game's fans for their contributions.

My friend from Jacksboro, Monroe Henderson, was already playing at Tech, and he and I signed with the Jacksboro

Roughnecks, who played on Saturday nights, and with the Midway Falcons, who played on Sunday afternoons. Earlier that spring, I thought I was on my way to athletic glory as a Texas A&M Aggie. However, I learned that Texas A&M was quite different from Jacksboro, where I had grown up loving my friends, my family, and baseball.

CHAPTER THREE
EXPERIENCES IN HIGHER EDUCATION

In the early spring of 1955, Jacksboro High School principal A. G. Beane asked me if I would consider playing football and baseball for his alma mater, Texas A&M University in College Station. Although I preferred baseball, the most talented college athletes played football in Texas then. They still do. In 1955, full baseball scholarships were extremely rare. Student-athletes often received half-baseball and half-football scholarships.

Principal Beane saw my potential as a combination football and baseball player, and he also thought that my friends Bobby Murray and Jim Boley could improve the A&M football team's previous year's losing record. In 1954 the Aggies only won one game, losing nine overall and six in conference play. That was also the first year Paul "Bear" Bryant became head coach. He was confident he could help the Aggies become a winning team. (Bryant later became famous at the University of Alabama as one of the greatest coaches of all time.)

Principal Beane sent our football films to A&M, along with our high school football and baseball statistics. My friends and I had earned some local and area honors, but we were not among the top prospects in the state. The A&M coaches liked what they saw in the films and offered both Bobby Murray and Jim Boley full football scholarships and me a half-football, half-baseball scholarship.

To prepare us to become Aggies, A&M invited us to their traditional High School Athletes' Week in College Station. We excitedly packed our jeans and letter jackets and squeezed into Bobby's old black pickup on a Friday afternoon. We turned out of Bobby's driveway and headed south to begin our six-hour trip to Aggieland.

Our parents had provided us with many roadmaps, all highlighted, for the journey from Jacksboro to College Station. Interstate 35 would have been perfect for our trip, but it was still under construction in 1955 and had numerous detours. When completed, I-35 would be called the "Main Street of Texas" because it links four of Texas's largest cities: Dallas, Fort Worth, Austin, and San Antonio. But in 1955 we traveled on small two-lane highways. Our parents packed us sack meals to eat en route, as there were no fast food restaurants.

Arriving late on Friday night, we were greeted by a few current students, including Jacksboro's own Paul Lillard, who was an all-state football player in 1953 and had become a guard for A&M. We were surprised to see Paul wearing a military uniform, and we soon discovered that all the students wore military uniforms because A&M was a military school. We also later realized that A&M did not allow any black students on campus, as all Texas universities were segregated at the time.

We were overwhelmed by the possibility of being Aggies, although we knew very little about the university. The next day we learned some aspects of the school that we did not appreciate. At dawn the bugles blared, and everyone scrambled to dress and go to breakfast. As we sleepily pulled on our jeans and T-shirts and staggered behind the rest of the cadets to the mess hall, three future Aggies started feeling distraught. We sat across the table from some freshmen, and they started eating at attention while upperclassmen constantly screamed at them. We could barely chew our food.

The day improved when we toured the football field and training rooms. We were soon enjoying A&M's spring football practices, dividing our time between them and watching A&M's baseball team play Rice, but we were more interested in the weight room. It amazed us.

We had never seen an official weight room, complete with exercise machines. We understood the concept behind lifting free weights, but we didn't know how the other machines worked. We were very impressed by them, but we were too embarrassed to act like we were impressed.

After watching football and baseball all day, we ate dinner in the athletes' cafeteria, where Coach Bryant would address us. He welcomed us to A&M, explaining its history and his plans to build the school's football program into a national powerhouse. His efforts were later rewarded because in the fall A&M's record improved to 7–2–1 overall and 4–1–1 in conference play.

After his speech, he asked us if we had any questions. There was silence. Any intelligent person would never have dared to ask the feared head coach a question, particularly in public. So, of course, I raised my hand.

"Yes, son?"

"I have something that's been troubling me since I got here. Where do they keep the girl students?" I asked.

Coach Bryant stared at me, a look of disbelief on his face. His mouth hung open for a moment, and he finally asked, "Son, where are you from?"

After I told him, he said, "There are no women at Texas A&M, and there never will be!"

Coach Bryant shook his head, and Bobby and Jim looked at the floor. I didn't know that A&M did not yet admit women students because it was a military school, and women did not serve in active duty in the armed forces in those days.

Our drive home the next day was unusually quiet. During that time we realized we'd probably never be Aggies.

Much to Principal Beane's disappointment, I applied to Texas Technological College (now Texas Tech University) in Lubbock late in the spring semester of my senior year. When I finally received my acceptance, all of the athletic scholarships were gone. Luckily, my friend Monroe Henderson, who had graduated from Jacksboro High School in 1953, was Texas Tech's starting shortstop. Monroe thought the baseball coaches would let me try out for their team and become a volunteer player, a "walk-on."

With the hope of playing baseball again, I began to look forward to starting school in Lubbock. There were many benefits to the university. At Tech I could be closer to home and enjoy going to classes with women students.

During the fall of 1955, my first semester at Texas Tech, my thoughts slowly turned to becoming a more serious baseball player. Tech, like A&M, placed a much greater emphasis on football than baseball, so most of my friends were football players. I lived in West Hall, Tech's dorm for athletes then, because the university assumed I'd be a scholarship baseball player in the spring.

My football player friends and I were extremely popular on campus. During my first semester, Tech's quarterback, Jack Kirkpatrick, rode his horse into the Student Union Building, tied the reins to the back of a chair, and ordered coffee. He was simply told to leave his horse outside next time.

In the 1950s, Tech was a sprawling, country school, and its remote location and extreme weather caused us to be very tolerant of each other. The weather in Lubbock ranged from sandstorms to snowstorms and made playing college sports difficult. The unbearable heat and dryness of August and September gave way to freezing temperatures in January, February, and March.

Baseball season finally arrived, and I felt like a real college athlete for the first time. After a few practices, the baseball coaches and players at Tech assured me that I was good enough to make the team and probably earn a starting position. I was excited at the possibility of being part of Tech's athletic department, the Red Raiders. The school had just been admitted to the famed Southwest Conference, which caused the students to form a huge conga line and dance in the streets, temporarily stopping traffic and shutting down businesses. On May 12, 1956, Tech's school newspaper, the *Daily Toreador*, ran the headline, "Extra! Finally! Tech Makes SWC, Tech Breaks SWC Jinx."

During the spring semester of 1956, I continued my workouts with the baseball team as a walk-on member. Being a walk-on meant that the coaches had no scholarship to offer me and no guarantee that they could find a scholarship for me, even if I played well and made the team.

My workouts were simply pitching to a catcher named Butch. Occasionally a coach would wander over and watch us. Butch and I could hardly wait to face some batters in a practice game. We wanted to know how we were going to fare in real combat.

I remember how excited I was when I received my Texas Tech uniform shortly before our first practice game. The jersey was light gray with black pinstripes and had the word "Raiders" across the chest in large, scarlet script. Our caps featured the famed "double T."

For our first practice game, West Texas State College came to Lubbock, and the coaches tried to give everyone a chance to play so that they could evaluate each player's potential. I patiently sat in the bullpen and nervously waited for my turn. After a few hours, I finally heard a shout from the dugout.

"Craft, warm up!"

Our pitcher was in trouble in the ninth inning. I thought I might get a chance to help him maintain our lead as I stood up and started throwing to Butch. Unfortunately, the pitcher managed to finish the game without my assistance, and I never made it out of the bullpen.

Following the game, we assembled in the Red Raider locker room for a team meeting. Coach Beattie Feathers stood to make announcements.

"I've decided to cut some players who aren't quite college material," he said. "I've posted their names on the bulletin board in the hallway outside my office. Those on the list, please turn in your uniforms."

As we crowded around the list, I gasped when I saw my name. Monroe was as shocked as I was. He put his arm around my shoulders and said, "Let's have a really good summer in semi-pro, and then we'll try again next spring."

"I didn't even play in a single game! How could he have done this to me without even giving me a shot at playing?" I asked Monroe.

Players circled me, commenting, "We don't get it either."

"Most teams keep a young pitcher, even if he needs time to develop."

"Good pitching's hard to find."

"Don't give up."

I turned in my uniform, placing it on a large pile with the others, all representing players who were suffering the same deep sorrow I felt. My dream of playing college baseball was gone, just like that highly coveted Red Raider uniform.

A rude dismissal from Tech's baseball team gave me the opportunity to focus on academics during the remainder of the spring semester, which helped me more than I'd like to admit. In fact, I made the Dean's List.

During the summer of 1956, I started playing for the same semi-professional ball teams I had been on in 1955: the Jacksboro Roughnecks and the Midway Falcons. Monroe was the starting shortstop, and I was a starting pitcher. After a few weeks into the season, a really good semi-pro team from Bowie noticed our play and recruited us, so we joined the Bowie team.

Bowie played in the Dry County League against teams from Nocona, Henrietta, Midway, Jacksboro, and Granbury. A "dry county" didn't have anything to do with a drought, though in the 1950s Texas suffered from a severe drought.

Instead, a dry county was one that did not sell alcohol. Teams in the Dry County League picked up players wherever they could. One player might say, "I met a guy in the oilfield the other day. He said he used to play semi-pro."

"What position?" we would ask. We were always looking for pitchers and catchers.

By the end of that summer, I was a seasoned semi-pro baseball veteran, two inches taller and thirty pounds heavier, measuring six foot two inches and 185 pounds. I could move quickly, and my fastballs were hopping.

Yes, I had matured physically, but mentally was another story. Tech's coaches visited me on campus in fall of 1956 and the winter of 1957, encouraging me to walk-on the baseball team again in the spring. I refused their offer.

Decades later I can admit that my wounded ego got the best of me, and I also disappointed Monroe, who wanted me to try out again. I would not even watch him play for Tech. Instead, I played intramural softball in the spring of 1957 and was named the All-College third baseman. Monroe continued to play varsity shortstop for the Red Raiders, was named team captain, and graduated from Texas Tech in May 1957.

After Monroe completed a solid college baseball career, he and I played in the Oil Belt League for the Cruise Tire Company in Wichita Falls for the summers of 1957 and 1958. We played most of our games at Spudder Park.

Monroe and I returned to the Oil Belt League for the summer of 1958. The league gave us blue jackets with a white and blue baseball emblem on the front that read, "Oil Belt League, Semi-Pro, 1958." I still have the emblem, moth-eaten and framed, hung in my office.

The summer passed quickly, and during the season's

last game, Monroe and I were named league all-stars. If that wasn't enough glory, the Cruise Tire Company awarded us each a set of tires for our fine performances.

As we were presented our tire coupons, a stranger approached us. He wore a straw hat and a neatly pressed white cotton dress shirt. He introduced himself as a scout from the Boston Red Sox and gave me his business card.

"Quite a game, Mr. Craft. Have you ever considered a career in professional baseball?" he asked me.

"No sir," I said. The thought had never crossed my mind, especially after I was cut from Tech's team.

"Why?" he asked.

"I don't think I'm good enough," I said.

"You most certainly are," he said. "Here is our standard contract. It doesn't have your name on it, but it shows you what your salary would be. I think you could play for the Red Sox."

I thanked him, and I couldn't think of anything else during the long drive back to Jacksboro. I rode with Monroe, and we talked about my major-league prospects. Monroe had already tried out for the Baltimore Orioles and the Washington Senators.

Monroe had told me after his tryout, "If you're really good, then you have to go for it. If you're not, then it's not a good life. You see," he added, "the farm teams travel in old, beat-up buses, and the players don't make much money."

"Monroe," I finally said, "I can't see myself riding around in a broken-down old bus, playing in small towns for a small paycheck and wasting five years of my life."

He smiled and said, "Let's get on with our lives. I'm sure

you'll eventually find a nice girl to marry, and then we'll have kids to go home to and ranches to make our living on. Until then, we could continue playing semi-pro baseball during the summers."

"Yeah, and a set of new tires for my truck isn't such a bad deal," I said.

While we were pleased that a scout had noticed me, we were confident that we had made the right decisions for our lives. We knew we would be friends for a long time.

Chapter Four
Becoming a Star

I n 1959 Mr. Sedberry and his catcher Alfred Ray had spent several Sundays scouting me as a pitcher for their ball club. Both scouts came to the conclusion that I was the pitcher they wanted for the next season.

The problem? How were they going to convince a white boy to play in an all-black league?

They had solved that problem by not telling me they were black when they contacted me. I was initially hesitant to play baseball with them, but after that first game, they knew they had found the perfect pitcher, and I knew I had found a great team. During our first season, we faced several challenges and shared many joys together, and I never regretted my decision to join them.

My next opportunity to play against the Blues occurred on July 18, 1959, in front of a large crowd in Abilene. I struck out fourteen Blues batters, and we won 6–0, my only semi-professional no-hitter. I still have the game ball, bearing the event, date, and score, "No Hitter, July 18, 1959, W. F. 6, Abilene Blues 0."

The Stars were winners with me. After games, Rabbit always said to me, "When you showed up, we felt like we were unbeatable. We were proud to have you."

After I played my first game with the Stars, my father had asked me, "Well, how was your game? Did you win? What was this new team like?"

"Well, hey, I got some news for you. They're a black baseball team, and they play in a black baseball league," I said.

"Surely you're not going to play with them again," he said.

"Yeah, I am. I enjoyed the game, and they have a really talented team," I said.

Because the Stars and I played baseball well together, we quickly started treating each other as teammates. I could see from their reactions to me when I arrived at our games that they were really happy to see me, but while we had baseball in common, our personal lives were very different.

Because we lived in such separate worlds, the Stars' and my shared passion for baseball had limits. Major League Baseball was another world to them, one that still lacked significant diversity. My teammates also disliked the way white players and fans in the majors could be hostile toward black players.

When I think back to 1959 and the transitions taking place in my country, in my life, and in the lives of those around me, I realize that I spent my first season with the Stars simply getting to know them. I'm still a little surprised they took the time to get to know me.

Their first probes into my personal life came during tailgating parties, the small social gatherings that occurred after games as we relaxed, surrounded by their families and friends. We would sit under trees to escape the Texas heat, or we would fold down the tailgate of a truck, sit on it, and dangle our feet over the side. They would chat about everyday events, and I would listen attentively.

In a June 1998 interview for the *Dallas Morning News*, Bryan Woolley referred to me as "Jackie Robinson in reverse," but during those days I never pictured myself like that. I was only ten years old when Robinson started playing for the Brooklyn Dodgers. I can't recall seeing him play for the Dodgers in 1947, the year he broke the color barrier in modern organized baseball. My family did not even own a television until 1950, the year I turned thirteen.

After we bought our first TV, I watched Robinson and read about him in the newspaper. He had natural ability on the field, intelligence, bearing, and good looks. His way of silencing his enemies was to keep his mouth shut. He let his playing skills speak volumes for himself.

I was not Jackie Robinson because I am a talker and a social person. I wanted the Stars to accept me not only as an athlete but also as a human being, a person worth knowing. I grew to know my team, especially Mr. Sedberry, as we sat on the bench watching baseball for two seasons.

Carl Sedberry, Jr., was born in Clifton, Texas, in 1933, where his father owned an auto body shop and a café. The junior Sedberry grew up working in both, but he told me that he liked working in his father's café much better. Carl Sr. was a fine infielder who coached the local black baseball team. He loved baseball and taught the strategies of the game to his son, who didn't have his father's athletic abilities.

In 1947 the family moved to Graham, Texas, and the senior Sedberry opened a barbecue place on Lincoln Street called Sedberry's Café. At that time young Carl attended the one-room school for blacks, Lincoln School. Two years later the white principal of Graham High School met with the Sedberry family and explained to them that their son would be the right student to integrate the public schools in Graham. The Sedberrys pondered this request for some time. Probably scared to death of the situation, the son told his parents that he simply did not want to go to school with all those white folks. His parents did not force the issue.

Instead, they decided that they could find a good school for their son without causing him to have a nervous breakdown. That meant Carl Sr. drove for two hours every Sunday, taking his son to an aunt's house in Fort Worth so that Carl Jr. could attend Terrell High School (founded in 1921 and originally named Fort Worth Colored High School), an all-black school. Each Friday the father returned to Fort Worth to pick up his son for the weekend. After graduating, Carl Jr. returned to Graham to work at the Graham Magnetics Company and at his family's café, which he later operated after his father retired.

Carl Jr.'s time in Fort Worth allowed him to experience life in a big city, coming into contact with many different kinds of people. Those contacts were useful to him when he became the manager of the Stars in 1953, dealing with other managers and players from various places, large and small.

Mr. Sedberry took pride in the Stars and always considered himself the team's manager, not its coach. "Coaches will tell you how to improve your game," he said. "I don't do that. Organization is my strength. Mainly, I just put the best players on the field and let them play."

He also kept a strict inventory of our equipment and

hauled everything to games. Our bats, balls, and bases were precious to him. He also had a little black book that held all the names and phone numbers of the Stars and other semi-pro teams in the area.

Although he was extremely busy managing us, he always made time to compliment me when I performed well. He'd tell me, "You have an above-average fastball, but you have the best curveball I've ever seen."

If I've been called "Jackie Robinson in reverse," then Mr. Sedberry can safely be called "the black Branch Rickey." Numerous ball players, both black and white, always referred to Branch Rickey, the white owner of the Brooklyn Dodgers who signed Jackie Robinson, as "Mr. Rickey," just as I showed respect to Mr. Sedberry by using his last name.

Similarly, major-league players respected Mr. Rickey because he organized and ran not only the Dodgers but also created a farm system that developed talented players for the major-league team. He saw the untapped potential talent in black players, and like Mr. Sedberry's sending Alfred to scout me in the white Oil Belt League, Mr. Rickey sent his scouts in search of talented players in the Negro Leagues. Mr. Sedberry's and Mr. Rickey's desire to win baseball games and willingness to integrate their teams caused immeasurable changes in the hearts and minds of those around them.

Mr. Sedberry's vision of an integrated Stars team led to wins at home and in Abilene against the Blues, but we were about to be tested on a tougher road trip. As we prepared to travel to Grandfield, Oklahoma, to play the Zebras, Mr. Sedberry told us the Zebras would be the best team we would face that summer.

We packed players and equipment into three full cars, eventually arriving at Grandfield in southwestern Oklahoma. The ballpark was at the end of a long, narrow dirt road, where I could see close to one thousand people waiting in the distance. As we approached them, we realized many members of the crowd were extremely short because the local black population included some people with dwarfism.

Mr. Sedberry then got out of his car and started searching for the Zebras' manager. When he couldn't find him, he asked a circle of tall Zebra players for help. The players widened their circle to reveal Nero, their tiny manager, sitting down in the middle of them, going over the lineup.

He was a feisty little man, and he yelled at Mr. Sedberry, "I'm down here! What do you want?" He was wearing a very small Zebra uniform, which sported alternating horizontal one-inch stripes of black-and-white material. The word "Zebras" was stitched in black across a white stripe on the uniform chests. The black-and-white stripes shifted around Mr. Sedberry, and we laughed as he bent down to talk to the manager.

We became quiet, though, as we watched the Zebras go through their warm-ups. I knew I'd have my hands full. Their pitcher was the best I'd seen or would ever see in the West Texas Colored League.

After seven innings, we became locked in a pitchers' duel, 3–3, when, with two outs, Nero decided to put himself in the game as a pinch hitter. He crouched down as low as he could and presented a strike zone of maybe twelve inches. I walked him, but the next batter hit a sharp grounder deep in the hole between second and third base. Our shortstop, Earnest "Fat" Locke, fielded it cleanly and easily threw Nero out at second as he headed toward the bag with little waddling steps. Our crowd couldn't help but laugh as the tiny manager ran toward second base.

Still tied at the top of the ninth, down to our last two outs, Mr. Sedberry called time and put in big Hubert "Bo" Beasley as a pinch hitter. He hit a fastball so far that it rolled past the crowd and into a stock tank, a small pond used to provide cattle with water.

Baseballs were valuable to both teams, but no one wanted to wade into the water to retrieve the ball. Mr. Sedberry laughed as the Zebra outfielders stood with the cows at the stock tank's edge, peering into the dark water.

A frustrated Zebra centerfielder then dove into the tank, retrieved the ball, and nearly threw Bo out at third. Without an outfield fence, the ball was still in play even when it was under water. Mr. Sedberry then ran out on the field and argued violently that it wasn't the same ball. He wanted a home run to put the Stars ahead, 4–3.

"Hey," he hollered at the umpire, "that could be any ball! Who knows how many balls are in that tank!"

The Grandfield umpire inspected the ball and declared that it was the same ball that Bo had hit, or close enough, and the tied game continued with Bo looking dejected at third.

Wayne Fisher was the next batter. He worked their pitcher to a 3–2 count and then hit a little opposite field blooper to put the Stars ahead 4–3 as Bo lumbered across home plate. I retired the bottom half of the ninth for the Stars' win.

Before we left Grandfield, I experienced my first away-game tailgating party. My teammates' wives always brought the food, especially an abundance of home-cooked fried chicken, which we always shared with the opposing team.

We sat on truck tailgates, bumpers of cars, or on folding chairs when they were available. Mostly the men visited with the men, and the women visited with the women. Sometimes small black children would stand near me, staring. I had to remind myself that they had never seen a white man play baseball with a black team and then stay to socialize afterward.

At the Grandfield tailgating party, my nickname of "white boy" changed in a significant way. Wayne Fisher had a number of friends and relatives in Grandfield, and he introduced me all around. He would put his arm around my shoulders and say, "This is *our* white boy, Jerry."

Wayne's introducing me to his family and friends as "our white boy" and using my first name was meaningful to me. I was touched.

We played Grandfield again the following Sunday at Spudder Park. Fans started arriving at noon for the 2:00 p.m. game, and Mr. Sedberry looked happy with the number in attendance.

"Well, Mr. Craft, I estimate we have about 1,500 in the stands," he said. "Let's not disappoint them."

We didn't. We were again tied 3–3 in the top of the ninth. The Zebras had runners on the corners with one out. The batter hit a grounder deep in the hole to Fat's right side. Fat fielded it smoothly and threw to second. Emmitt Johnson tagged second and relayed the ball to Fisher at first for a close double play. The runner was safe.

Mr. Sedberry protested mightily, but to no avail. The run scored, and we trailed by one run going into the bottom of the ninth.

Two outs later all hope seemed lost, but Rabbit hit a double to right field. Bo Beasley was up next, and we cheered for the two-out rally. Bo hit the first pitch to deep center field for the final out. We had just lost the game, our last opportunity to play the Zebras that year. Mr. Sedberry said that neither team would schedule another game because no one wanted to lose again. Our 4–3 loss to Grandfield at home was our only loss of the 1959 season, my favorite season with the Stars.

After our games against Grandfield, I started to feel that the Stars had accepted me, but we faced the challenge of playing more away games. Mr. Sedberry would call me a day or two before a road trip because we had to carpool. I always brought my 1958 bronze-colored Chevrolet Impala convertible, and I welcomed whoever joined me. Usually Rabbit, Alfred, and Bo rode with me, but that sometimes changed because we never knew who would need a ride.

When we were all assembled, Mr. Sedberry led the way in his car. Many of the luxuries we take for granted on road trips were not available in those days. We had no fast-food restaurants and no food "to go." Instead, we each took our own sack lunch and ate it on the road. When we got hungry, we stopped at gas stations that served whites only, and I went inside to buy the entire team cold drinks and chips while my teammates waited outside.

My teammates did not seem upset by this arrangement. I think they were happy that I was along so that they could have cold drinks, which were a real luxury for my team.

We got plenty of rude stares during those stops at gas stations, but I don't remember anyone asking me what I was doing. I was obviously a part of a team. We were all wearing uniforms, so observers knew we were going somewhere to play baseball.

We sometimes tried to avoid stopping at gas stations by topping off our gas tanks before we left town. There simply weren't as many gas stations as today, and we took our chances on running out of gas every time we passed one. I don't remember any stations refusing to sell gas to me for our team, though they could have easily done so.

During those road trips, we would have to stop to use the restroom. Those stops were complicated because my black teammates could not use the whites-only public restrooms. Instead, we'd have to pull down a side road or a country lane.

When someone needed to stop, one of the players in Mr. Sedberry's car at the front of the caravan signaled us by holding his cap out the window. We carefully chose abandoned country lanes because we couldn't risk being reported to the law.

On the road trips I got to know Clarence Elbert "Rabbit" Myles, who is still my good friend. Although he could have fun, he was a serious competitor and the most reliable of my teammates. I knew that Rabbit would always come to my defense.

While Mr. Sedberry, Fat, and Rabbit got to know me and like me, right-fielder Bobby Lee Herron never seemed to accept me. He never adopted "our white boy" as a term of endearment for me.

Bobby always sat on the far left-hand side of the bench, rarely conversing with anyone. I assumed that Bobby didn't care for me because I was white and therefore an intrusion.

Years later, though, Rabbit and Mr. Sedberry assured me that Bobby didn't particularly care for anyone.

As the least social of the Stars, Bobby wasn't exactly mean or rude to me. He just kept to himself, mentally and physically, though he mellowed a little with age. Before Bobby died in 2002, he, Rabbit, and I sat in the dugout at the Jacksboro High School Baseball Field for an interview with John Pronk from a Dallas TV station.

When Bobby had finished talking, I pointed out that just as in his days with the Stars, he was still sitting away from the rest of us, on the far end of the bench.

While Bobby remained quiet around me, most of my teammates, like Fat, Fisher, and Rabbit, had accepted me. However, our team was still missing a close camaraderie that most teams enjoy. A road trip to Waco, Texas, gave us a traumatic experience and common ground that connected us all.

The Southwestern Bell African American History Month Family
Day and Negro League Baseball Reunion (Southwest) at the African
American Museum in Dallas at Fair Park on February 20, 1999.
From left to right are James Williams (who played for a
different team managed by Mr. Sedberry), Jerry Craft,
Mr. Sedberry, and Jerry's teammate Clarence "Rabbit" Myles.

Jacksboro's Old Town Team—circa 1931. Left to right in front row: Masters Randolph and Bert Noel, bat boys; second row: J. D. Craft, Harry Key Turner, Jess Massengale, Claude Gregg, Peck Wade, Shine Myers, Pat Patoosis; back row: John K. Hackley, Pete Simons, Chet Brummet, Darrell Lester, Wallace Myers (Jerry's future high-school baseball coach), Red Stoddard, and Bones Risley.

Jerry Craft's thirteenth birthday party in 1950 with his baseball friends. Left to right in front row: Linda Craft, Nick Sikes, Jerry (holding the cake), Jim Boley, Richard Teague, and Tony Clark. The back row includes Keith Patton and Don Massengale.

Jerry Craft in 1953 on the Jacksboro High School football team. Helmets at that time did not have facemasks; the injury to his left eye, from playing with a pocketknife as a child, is clearly visible. Courtesy Jacksboro High School, Jacksboro, Texas.

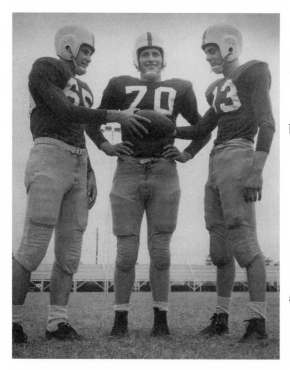

Jim Boley, Bobby Murray, and Jerry Craft, the tri-captains of the 1954 Jacksboro High School football team. Each Jacksboro player picked his own number, which confused opposing offenses and defenses. The 1954 team became the District 9–AA District Champions. No yearbook photos exist of the baseball team because the baseball season started after the deadline for printing the yearbooks. Courtesy Jacksboro High School, Jacksboro, Texas.

J. D. Craft, center, in 1955 at the Will Rogers Coliseum in Fort Worth, Texas. He and his favorite horse, Miss Texas, have just been named champions of a cutting-horse contest at the Fat Stock Show.

Jerry Craft's high-school graduation photo in 1955. He and fifty-four other students graduated that year, earning the nickname "55 in '55." Jerry was an honor graduate and president of the Jacksboro High School's chapter of the National Honor Society. Courtesy Jacksboro High School, Jacksboro, Texas.

Monroe "Mo" Henderson fielding a baseball as shortstop for Texas Technological College (now Texas Tech University) in Lubbock in spring 1957. He was varsity baseball team captain at Texas Tech during the 1956 and 1957 seasons and a three-year letterman (1955, 1956, and 1957). His batting average his senior year was .346. Courtesy Monroe Henderson.

The 1959–60 All-College Football Champions of Texas Technological College, Sigma Alpha Epsilon Fraternity, with Jones Stadium in the background. Left to right in front row: Jerry Craft, Bob Tinney, Delbert Bassett, Warner Phillips, Jack Lalament, Malcolm Garrett, Dick Phelps. Back row: Jimmy Johnson, Daryl Summers, Bob Kinney, Jerry Pearson, Jimmy Williams, and Gordon Richardson.

Linda Craft with her golf clubs in 1983. She was a member of the LPGA from 1967 until 1973. She and Penny Zavichas created the Craft-Zavichas Golf School in Pueblo, Colorado, in 1968 to help women learn to play golf. The school is still in operation.

Earnest "Fat" Locke and wife, Catherine (Cat), on their wedding day. They were married in June 1951 at the Mount Calvary United Methodist Church in Wichita Falls, Texas. Courtesy Sandra Contreras.

Earnest "Fat" Locke in his bus driver uniform. He drove a bus for the city of Wichita Falls, Texas, from January 1999 until his death on July 30, 2004. Previously he was a salesman at Nunn's Electric in Wichita Falls until his retirement in December 1998. Courtesy Sandra Contreras.

Clarence "Rabbit" Myles and wife, Arnita, on their wedding day on May 30, 1959. They were married in Graham, Texas, at the home of Arnita's father, James Campbell. Courtesy Clarence Myles.

Coach Clarence "Rabbit" Myles, far left, and his basketball team for the Boys and Girls Clubs in Wichita Falls, Texas, in 1981–1982. On the front row, second from left, is his son Melvin; front row, far right, is his son, Clarence, Jr. Rabbit coached Boys and Girls Clubs teams for twenty-nine years, touching hundreds of young lives. Courtesy Clarence Myles.

Carl Sedberry, Jr., at the Dallas African American Museum in 1999 at a reunion of former players. He appeared on a panel under the theme "Triumph Over Adversity" narrated by historian Larry Lester. Courtesy NoirTech Research, Inc.

Jerry Craft spent two years as a pitcher for the Wichita Falls/Graham Stars as the first white player in the West Texas Colored Baseball League. Photograph by Gary Lawson; originally published on the front page of the *Wichita Falls Times Record News* (November 23, 2005, vol. 99, no. 165).

Jerry Craft and wife Pamela celebrating Thanksgiving with family on the Craft Ranch in Jacksboro, Texas, 2006.

CHAPTER FIVE
WELCOME TO OUR WORLD,
WHITE BOY

When Mr. Sedberry announced a July 1959 road trip to Waco, Texas, to play the Tigers, I turned to Fat and said, "Hey, this is our fourth weekend on the road. Spudder Park is, by far, the finest stadium in the league. Why are we always on the road?"

"White boy, we know everyone in Wichita Falls," he said. "We like to travel so that we can meet new people."

The Stars looked forward to socializing at away games, beginning with our ride-sharing. Mr. Sedberry organized four cars, including his, Rabbit's, mine, and Fat's, for the Waco trip. Mr. Sedberry's car broke down about an hour outside of town. The frustrated players piled into two cars, mine and Rabbit's, because Fat would not allow us in his car for away games. He always had a girlfriend with him. The ride was terribly uncomfortable, people and equipment stuffed everywhere, but we had no choice. No white mechanic would work on a black person's car on a Sunday, or probably any other day, and we knew no black mechanics nearby. We left the broken-down car by the side of the road.

We arrived in Waco more than an hour late. The heat and crowded traveling conditions caused us to be in a foul mood. When we found out we were playing on a very recently used cow pasture, we felt even worse. Dry and not-so-dry piles of cow manure decorated the infield dirt. We found shovels and paper plates, and both teams scooped the manure off the infield.

The rest of the field was also in bad shape. I noticed right away that the infield did not have a pitcher's mound. Instead, an ancient rubber pitcher's plate sat directly on the flat ground. The edges of the rubber crumbled into the dirt.

Once we had cleared the infield, I walked toward the outfield to investigate the condition of the grass. I didn't get very far because giant weeds, at least two feet high, stretched into the next county. No outfield fence stopped them, and I did not understand how our outfielders were going to chase fly balls through those weeds.

As the Stars roamed the field, complaining loudly about its condition, more than five hundred Waco fans had arrived. Our car trouble and work on the infield had delayed the start of the game, but the crowd didn't care because that meant they had extra time to socialize. The fans laughed and joked with each other, feeling very festive as they sat around the edges of the cow pasture on warped bleachers.

Because the field had no bullpen, I walked across the infield to the rotting rubber marker to begin my warm-ups. The first time I stood on the marker and pushed off, it tore apart.

"Mr. Sedberry!" I yelled and pointed to the broken pieces at my feet.

"Whoo boy!" he characteristically proclaimed. Mr. Sedberry's favorite expression in critical times was always "Whoo boy!"

"What else can go wrong today?" he added. He shouldn't have asked.

He waved to the Tigers' manager and explained the problem. The manager, a very large, pleasant man, filled every inch of his oversized uniform. The manager then called the Tigers' team captain to the broken rubber marker.

"I have a tool box in my trunk with some hammers and long bridge nails," he said, handing the captain a key. "We'll get this thing fixed."

"What is this 'we'?" the captain asked. "I is the captain, and I don't do that sort of thing. You fix it yourself!" He gave the key back to the manager.

The manager instantly stood toe-to-toe with the captain and announced, "I is the manager. I give the orders on this team. Now, you go get that toolbox!" He shoved the key back in the captain's hands.

The captain then ran to the car's trunk, unlocked it, and grabbed one large tool, a combination hammer and hatchet. He let out a scream and ran toward the manager like a Comanche with his tomahawk drawn back.

Mr. Sedberry and I stood back with our mouths open as the very large target of a manager ran for his life. Then the Stars all sprinted for the safety of our benches. We stood behind them to view the fight.

The fans delighted in the unexpected entertainment. As the manager and captain circled the bases, I told Mr. Sedberry, "He's trying to hurt that man! Shouldn't we call the sheriff to come out here?"

"Good grief, Mr. Craft," he replied, staring at me in disbelief. "Do you really think the police would drive out to this cow pasture on a Sunday afternoon to keep our baseball teams from hurting each other?"

"Well, I hadn't thought of it in that way before, but I guess you're right," I said.

Our attention returned to the field, where the fight continued. As the manager and the captain started around the bases a second time, the captain tripped over first base, fell, and lost his weapon. The manager, now exhausted, grabbed a bat and screamed, "Now YOU better move!"

They started their third trip around the bases, this time with the manager in pursuit of the captain. After they ran the bases two more times, both fell exhausted. The appreciative audience brought them refreshments, and after a short rest, the manager and captain started repairing the pitching rubber together like nothing had happened.

The Stars then started to relax and talk among themselves freely, but I really didn't want to stay in Waco after seeing the Tigers fight each other.

"Mr. Sedberry, why don't we just go home?" I asked.

"No, we traveled all the way here, and the fans want to see a game. We should play," he replied.

I slowly nodded my head, but the fight had distracted me. The Tigers took an early lead. In addition, our usually reliable outfield showed no hustle. Between innings I asked Rabbit what was wrong with them.

"Snake holes," he replied.

"Snake holes?" I asked.

"Yep, all over the outfield. We are scared to death of

rattlesnakes," Rabbit said as we walked together toward the field. "There," he pointed to a hole dug among the weeds. "There's a snake hole."

"Ah, Rabbit," I said. "That's just an armadillo hole."

"How do you know the difference?" he asked.

"I'm a country boy," I said. "I know." But he continued to stare at the hole from a safe distance.

"Well, country boy, do rattlesnakes sometimes live in armadillo holes?" he asked.

That was a good question. I hesitated. "Yes, they sometimes do," I said. He glared at me, but I quickly added, "I'm quite sure no snakes live in those holes." The crowd was becoming impatient with our team meeting and hole inspection.

"If you're so sure no snakes live there, you put your arm in that hole," Rabbit told me, but I declined.

"Let's do our best to keep the ball in the infield," I told my teammates. I returned to the mound and told the infield, "I'll pitch the ball low, so watch for ground balls."

Amazingly, we won that game with an extremely slow outfield, but we didn't want to stay for our usual postgame visit. We were not comfortable in Waco and quickly made plans to return home.

Mr. Sedberry then suggested we have supper in West, Texas, a small town north of Waco founded by Czechoslovakian immigrants. I asked Mr. Sedberry if any of the restaurants in West would serve our team. "We're going to be fine!" he laughed. "It's a black café, Mr. Craft. I've eaten there several times."

When we finally arrived at the small café, we were very

tired and hungry. Our team eagerly anticipated an unexpected treat, sitting down together and ordering a good meal at a public restaurant.

I dropped off my teammates at the door and parked the car. Because of the heat, they didn't wait for me. They went into the restaurant and ordered huge amounts of food. When I walked in several minutes later, I noticed some of the black diners staring at me, but I thought little of it.

The Stars teased me again about the snake holes. I was happy to be included in their conversation. As soon as I relaxed, the restaurant owner came over to my table, leaned over, and said softly to me, "Sir, I don't want any trouble, but you are going to have to leave."

"Why?" I asked.

"Because you are white, and my customers don't want you here," he said.

At first Mr. Sedberry ignored the exchange and asked me why I hadn't ordered my food yet. I tried to respond to Mr. Sedberry, but I was interrupted.

"We're not going to serve this man," the owner told Mr. Sedberry.

Mr. Sedberry was instantly out of his seat and at my side, protesting as if the restaurant owner were an umpire who had made a terribly bad call. "This man is a member of my baseball team," he told the café owner. "We are hungry, and he is trying to place an order."

"It don't make any difference who he is," the owner replied. "He is white, and he has to leave. The rest of your team can stay."

"We are a team! We play together as a team, we travel together as a team, and we eat together as a team," Mr. Sedberry responded. He was in shock because he never expected such treatment in a place that had always been friendly toward him and the Stars.

All the food the team had ordered began arriving at our table, and we were really hungry. Mr. Sedberry looked at all the plates of food on the table and looked at me. I couldn't believe what was happening.

Rabbit later told me that he was just as surprised as Mr. Sedberry. He explained the situation to me this way: "I could understand if you'd been a black man going into a white restaurant because I'd seen that happen when I lived in San Antonio. You couldn't get served in a white restaurant if you was black. The black man had to go in back doors to get something to eat."

Mr. Sedberry then took a deep breath and turned away from the owner. He sat down and said calmly to me and the team, "Let's eat." That strategy was not going to work. The owner would not back down.

"Not here you won't!" he yelled.

"If Jerry doesn't eat, then we don't eat!" Mr. Sedberry yelled back. Mr. Sedberry then turned toward the door and clenched his fists. I had never seen him so angry. To a man, the hungry team stood up and walked away from plates full of food. The door was slammed and locked behind us.

I stood in the bright Texas sun, stunned, trying to understand what was happening to me. Bobby Herron walked up beside me, put his left arm around my shoulders, and with a rare, large grin said, "Welcome to our world, white boy!"

I realized that Bobby was delighted to see a white person experience the humiliation that he and his teammates had endured for years. Then Alfred jumped up as if he was afraid. I looked around to see what had made him jump. A West police car rolled into the parking lot. The café's owner, apparently fearing retaliation, had called the police.

The cop was a stereotypical small-town southern law-enforcement officer of the late 1950s. He knew we were trouble, and he was going to keep his town safe.

"What you boys up to?" he asked, using the word "boys" in exactly the way my teammates hated it. The way he said it robbed us of our dignity, making us feel inferior to him even though we were adult men. We slowly backed toward our cars.

"We're leaving, sir, just like the man asked us to," I told him.

"What you doing here?" the cop asked me, looking me up and down.

"I play baseball with them, sir," I said.

He looked surprised and sneered, "I'm sure your folks are real proud of you."

I knew better than to say anything back to him. I feared he would put us all in jail if I tried to defend my teammates. He then stepped over to Rabbit's car, leaned on the window, and said to Rabbit, "Get out."

"Get out for what?" Rabbit asked.

"Get out," he repeated.

Then Rabbit got angry and started talking. If he hadn't said anything, he might not have been arrested, but talking to a white cop meant he would go to jail.

"Boy, I'm going to have to arrest you," he said to Rabbit,

and he handcuffed my friend and took him to jail. The Stars were stunned. We saw the patrol car drive away, Rabbit in the backseat. He glanced sheepishly at us, probably knowing he shouldn't have said anything. We had to get Rabbit out of jail before we went home.

We couldn't leave our friend in West, so we started searching our pockets, our bags, and our car seats for spare change. Gathering everything we had, probably a little less than fifty dollars, we went to the jail. Mr. Sedberry and I asked if we could pay Rabbit's fine.

"How much do you have?" the jailer asked. When we told him, he said that wasn't enough.

"It's all we have," I explained.

"Well, I guess that will do," the jailer sighed, as he stuck the cash in his pocket and unlocked Rabbit from his solitary cell. "Now, I don't want to see any of you boys around here ever again. We don't have room in our jail for an entire baseball team," he said.

His message was clear, and the Stars never returned to West. We drove home, quiet, broke, and hungry. I was still in shock as I traveled back to Jacksboro with my silently starving teammates.

A few days after my trip to Waco with the Stars, Jacksboro had a long late-afternoon rain. Rain in West Texas always puts ranchers in a good mood, especially a summer rain, so my father and I decided to sit on the front porch together and enjoy the weather. We sipped iced tea while my mother fixed supper.

To my surprise, my father asked about the game in Waco,

and I told him about the snake holes. Encouraged by his interest in my team, I told him what happened after the game.

"Then I got kicked out of a black restaurant in West, and one of my teammates got arrested," I continued. That was probably too much information for my father. He became very angry.

"Why, he had no right to kick you out of there!" he said.

"Don't you imagine that black fathers feel the same way when their sons are dragged out of public places?" I asked him.

He stared at me for a minute, and then we sat in silence. "Can I get you another iced tea, son?" he finally asked. He stood up and walked to the kitchen.

Even with his back to me, I could tell that he had softened slightly. He may not have agreed with me or with how I was spending my summer, but as a father, he understood a man's desire for his son to be treated fairly. Because he no longer wanted to talk about it, I thought that maybe he was considering my perspective.

When he came back with my drink, the conversation turned to Major League Baseball, something we always enjoyed discussing. He loved the game and knew team statistics much better than I did. We discussed every aspect of the game, from pitchers' records, RBIs, home runs, and batting averages, to stolen bases.

Mostly, however, we talked about the pennant races. I eagerly anticipated them and the World Series because even the ranching chores were put on hold during those games. We watched our favorite teams, the Yankees, Dodgers, and

Red Sox. My father, strangely enough, viewed the black ball-players in the same statistical category as the white players, meaning that if they played well enough, then they were OK. He was slowly accepting blacks as baseball players, and I knew this was progress for him. It was progress for all of us, but it didn't come rapidly or easily.

CHAPTER SIX
MR. SEDBERRY'S STARS

I n a small town like Jacksboro, it's hard to keep your personal life private. If my friends saw me in my Stars uniform at the root beer drive-in on Live Oak Street, they would ask, "Who are the Stars?" I explained to them that the Stars were a black baseball team, and we played throughout West and Central Texas, and sometimes even in Oklahoma.

"Why are you playing for a black team?" they asked me.

"When we were younger, we all played baseball with Jacksboro's black kids. What I am doing now really isn't much different, though we are a little older," I explained. "It's like pick-up games for adults, though having a league makes it a bit more organized." Then my friends smiled, nodded, and thought nothing of it.

While my friends eventually accepted my decision to play for the Stars, I realized that my father had never watched me play and probably never would. A few times during those years, I felt his absence. If had I urged him to watch us, I knew the answer would always be no.

Working on my father's ranch kept my arm strong. Sometimes I'd arrive at the ballpark completely worn out, feeling as if I couldn't pitch two innings, and then I'd pitch a brilliant game. Other times, I'd arrive fresh, rested, and raring to go, and then the other team would hit every one of my pitches.

Regardless, I always approached each game the same way. I would be positive, poised, and confident. I don't think I was ever arrogant, certainly not when I was playing with and against black ball clubs. They had plenty of arrogance already, and I think neither the opponents nor the Stars would have tolerated any arrogance from a white boy, no matter how talented he was.

Mr. Sedberry would play any team, anywhere. He once got a call from the manager of a Hispanic team from Eastland, Texas, the Hombres. Their manager had heard we were really good, so he told Mr. Sedberry the Hombres wanted to host us for a game. Mr. Sedberry scheduled our first game against them on a Sunday.

We knew that the Hombres had an undefeated season, but we soon discovered that the team was not as good as its record. We beat them quite handily, humiliating them on their home field.

The Eastland team became very resentful, especially when they witnessed the end of their undefeated season. After the game, their players and fans started taunting us and followed us to our cars. As we quickly drove away, we heard rocks hitting our cars. My teammates' cars had souvenir dents from the game, but, luckily, the rocks missed mine. The Stars didn't seem to mind the dents. I didn't think it was so funny.

"They can sure throw rocks better than they can throw baseballs!" Rabbit laughed.

Eastland's manager called the next night to see what time

we would play the following Sunday. Mr. Sedberry refused the Hombres' invitation, which angered their coach. He felt insulted that we were not giving his team a chance to beat us in a rematch.

The other all-Hispanic team we played was the Wichita Falls Lobos, which, like the Hombres, was not a member of the West Texas Colored League. The Lobos, a good defensive team for a group who played regularly on the weekends, lacked pitching and power hitting. I hit my only home run in Spudder Park off them. There was no one on base, and I knew that I had hit the ball very hard, but I couldn't see the ball fly through the bright Sunday afternoon sky.

I ran hard around first, looked up, and saw their players looking down, kicking the dirt. I stopped halfway to second, assuming I had hit a foul ball. I started to return to the plate when the field official said, "Son, where are you going? You just hit a home run!"

So, I sheepishly rounded the bases and entered the dugout to the laughter of my teammates. "Well, white boy, is it so rare for you to hit a home run that you forgot how to run the bases?" Fat laughed.

My teammates told me the shot was just inside the foul pole line, a 350-foot home run. I was proud of it anyway.

I remember the Stars' next road trip. It was my first time to play in Mineral Wells against the Fort Wolters Helicopter Base team. Fort Wolters began as a National Guard Training Center in 1921, but it was renamed Camp Wolters during World War II. The Air Force reactivated Camp Wolters in 1951 to train aviation engineers. In 1956 the camp changed hands yet again when the Army established Fort Wolters, a Primary Helicopter Training Center/School.

When Mr. Sedberry called the recreation director at Fort Wolters to schedule baseball games there, he had to specify whether he wanted to play the black team or the white team. Although the military had integrated, the baseball teams at Fort Wolters had not. Mr. Sedberry always wanted to play both teams, but he told me that the black team was by far the better of the two.

One Wednesday night in 1959 the black team from Fort Wolters traveled to play us in Graham. They had a terrific pitcher whose fastball was really on fire. He was probably one of the toughest pitchers I ever faced. In fact, I hit his fastball so hard that night it never got higher than four feet off the ground, straight to right-center field, where it wedged into the bull-wire fence.

Bull wire is heavy gauged and tightly woven, two capital-letter Vs facing opposite directions. It makes a good outfield fence because it's very strong when stretched and welded to metal cemented posts. Bull wire is so strong that it will turn back a bull, which is why it's called bull wire.

Their outfielders couldn't pull my ball out of the wire Vs. They stood there jabbing at it with their gloves. I had scored easily, but the umpires called me back to second for a ground rule double. If the ball hits the fence or the ground before it goes over the fence, the batter cannot advance past second base. That was the hardest ball I ever hit. It may still be jammed in that fence.

We were about halfway through our first season together

when we traveled to Haskell to face their black team, the Yellow Dogs. The team was named after and sponsored by a barbeque place west of Haskell, the Yellow Dog Tavern. Their team uniforms were white and had the words "Yellow Dogs" across the front in yellow.

We enjoyed playing Haskell because their baseball skills were good, but their food was better. They couldn't beat us, but boy, could they cook. Our entire team looked forward to the postgame meal.

The Tavern was about three miles away from the Yellow Dogs' field, a cow pasture with no lights and no fence. In fact, most of the fields we played on had no fences. The runner simply had to beat the throw home for a home run. After a game on a hot summer day, I greatly anticipated driving the dirt road to the Tavern. As soon as I opened the car door, I could smell the brisket, ribs, and chicken from the smoker.

The Tavern's old, unpainted frame building nestled in some large elm and cottonwood trees. Beneath them lay a few tables and benches, a collection of graying boards, almost skeletal in the bright sun. The family that owned the Tavern lived in its basement.

The Tavern consisted of one large room, which was both the kitchen and dining room. A large evaporative box cooler (an early method of air conditioning) sat in a corner, making more noise than cool air. The tables and chairs were constructed of old two-by-four lumber, and the worn wooden floors were stained from spilled barbeque. If we sat near the cooler, we couldn't hear the conversation from the other side of the table. That corner of the Tavern was generally reserved for several old, nearly deaf black men who spent most of their afternoons shouting at each other over the noise.

We always sat on the benches and tables outside. The women sat inside and visited, where they used worn hand fans to circulate the warm air. The fans were provided by the local funeral home. The kids ran in and out, slamming the screen doors and letting the flies in.

The Stars and Yellow Dogs enjoyed some very pleasant afternoons together at the Tavern. While we were sitting in the shade of the large trees at the Tavern savoring the bar-beque smells, Fat, the boldest of my teammates, asked me a personal question, the first I had heard from anyone. "White boy, Carl says you go to college. What's college like?"

The question and the use of Mr. Sedberry's first name surprised me. I sat quietly for a few minutes while I thought of a response. There were no black students at Texas Tech at the time. I became ashamed and embarrassed about being a college student, as I realized that for my teammates, thinking about attending college was about as remote as the idea of going to the moon.

Instead of talking with the Stars about the lack of black students, I decided to describe Lubbock, which none of my teammates had ever seen. I told them it was flat and treeless, surrounded by cotton fields, which caused some laughter. "Yes, we all know about cotton!" someone said. I smiled and blushed. We were trying to establish some common ground.

I told them how spread out the college grounds were and about the dust storms, the steam-heating systems for the buildings, and the number of students who attended the school.

"Are there any black students?" Bobby Lee Herron want-ed to know.

"No, there aren't," I told him.

The Yellow Dogs were also listening to me. Then they started asking me questions too. They wanted to know if I was married and how many cows I owned. I told them I was not married and estimated the number of cows and horses on our ranch. They shook their heads in disbelief at the size of our herds.

After they had an opportunity to ask me questions, I felt very accepted by the Yellow Dogs, who seemed to be much more interested in my cows and horses than in my college life. College was totally beyond their experience, but they understood farm animals and gardens.

I learned to talk to them about everyday things, like what I had gathered from my mother's garden the day before.

"White people have gardens?" asked Fat, shaking his head in disbelief. They thought that having a garden meant a family couldn't afford to buy food at the store.

I tried to explain. "Food tastes better when my mother grows it at home. She and I enjoy spending time in the garden."

Fat's gardening question and my answer began one of our longest and most animated conversations. Everyone had an opinion of what to grow in a garden and how to grow it.

When the Yellow Dogs would travel to play us, we always played them in Graham, not Wichita Falls, so that we could host them at Mr. Sedberry's Café. Mr. Sedberry challenged himself to provide the Yellow Dogs with food that was equal to the Tavern's. He did his best by closing his café on Lincoln Street on game evenings to everyone except the Yellow Dogs and their families and cooking barbeque for them.

Those meals are some of my favorite memories of my

two seasons with the Stars. I thought about my conversations with the Stars, especially about how my college was segregated. I began to feel sorry for my teammates' plight. They would not have the education I would, even when Texas Tech was finally integrated in 1961, because most of them couldn't afford tuition. I was becoming aware of the opportunities that I had always taken for granted, and that realization made a lasting impression on me.

As I neared the end of my first season with the Stars, I began to anticipate road trips and understand our interactions with other teams, especially white ones. The Windthorst Trojans were a very competitive semi-pro team of German immigrant dairy farmers. The only white team we knew who enjoyed baseball as much as we did, the Trojans were kinder to us than other white teams. Perhaps Windthorst's status as an immigrant community made its members more sympathetic to outsiders.

Our game against them started at 3:00 in the afternoon, but during the third inning, the Windthorst team called an unusual timeout, and several of their best players began to walk off the field.

"We have to go milk. We'll be back," they said to Mr. Sedberry as they waved goodbye to him. He nodded.

"What?" I asked him. "You're going to let them do that?"

"We have to allow substitutions in the game so those players can go home and milk their cows. They milk their cows three times a day, game or no game," he said.

I had never seen anything like it. Several of their best players simply left the game, intending to return later. Under the regular rules of baseball, once a player, like a pitcher, is pulled from a game, he may not play for the remainder of the game.

As the players left the field and the substitutes started warming up, I asked Mr. Sedberry what we were supposed to do.

"Oh, Mr. Craft, we'll keep playing. They got plenty of players to use as substitutes. We have to let a few of them go milk, though. We can wait, but those cows can't," he said.

A few weeks later, Mr. Sedberry and my teammates wanted a Fourth of July game, but we couldn't find anyone to play us. So, he called the manager of the Windthorst team, and they agreed to a game. He told Mr. Sedberry they'd be happy to come to Graham if we'd provide the barbeque for their families. Mr. Sedberry said he'd be happy to provide the food by hauling the smoker to the ballpark.

The Windthorst team and fans enjoyed celebrating America's independence in Graham. We won the game because most of the Windthorst substitutes stayed home to milk the cows, but that seemed secondary to both teams that day. We ate and watched the children play together in the late afternoon sun. At dark we turned off the stadium lights and put on a fireworks display for them.

Earlier in the day I had taken off the blouse that I wore under my jersey because it was quite warm. That evening I was still wearing my old white cotton jersey when a strong wind from the south caused some of the children's sparklers to sputter and fade, flashing on and off in the dark like fireflies. I volunteered to help, and they all gathered around me as I turned my back to the wind and began to light their sparklers again. One small black child's sparkler burst into unexpectedly bright sparks. Startled, he thrust it away from himself and into my jersey. I ran screaming around the infield while the children chased me. They laughed and clapped for me when I finally stopped running to drop and roll out the flames.

The Stars talked about that Fourth of July for a long time. Mr. Sedberry and I kept recalling the white kids and the black kids playing together while their parents socialized near them. This was unheard of at that time.

"Maybe, just maybe, times are beginning to change," Mr. Sedberry said to me. "Who would have thought that the Germans would be the ones?"

"Yes, that is ironic," I agreed.

For the last game of my first season with the Stars, we faced our buddies from Haskell, the Yellow Dogs, at home in Graham. We played them on a Sunday afternoon, the last weekend in August. The victory was bittersweet, capping a 31–1 season, because I knew that a very special summer in my life had come to an end. After the game, we socialized at Mr. Sedberry's Café with our usual barbeque.

We talked about what an exceptional year we had shared. No one could remember winning thirty-one games in one season. We never kept individual statistics, but I knew my won-loss record was 16–1.

I told my friends and teammates goodbye that day because I would be leaving soon to return to Texas Tech and needed to pack for school. Each one of them asked if I would play again next summer. I said yes, and some of us shook hands. I promised I'd be back, and I kept my promise.

CHAPTER SEVEN
SECOND SEASON

I returned to Texas Tech in the fall of 1959 for my final year in college. Although my college days were collectively the happiest days of my young life, I missed baseball and the Stars. I looked forward to the next summer, 1960, when I could play for them again.

Mr. Sedberry and I spoke on the phone during my Christmas break. We talked about his work, my school, and our teammates. He encouraged me to make good grades, and I told him I was studying as often as possible.

During the holidays, Mr. Sedberry also sent me a Christmas card. I showed it to my folks. It meant so much to me that I still have it. The front of the card depicts a black family gathered around a roaring fire, a lavishly decorated Christmas tree beside them. The well-dressed, handsome parents hand presents to their beautiful, beaming children. A set of grandparents watch the festive occasion from a comfortable couch in the corner. The card includes the following message, "Love, Carl, Mary, Dorene, and D.C."

My father gently turned it over and said, "Golly, if it weren't for the fact that they are all black, it looks just like any other family at Christmas!"

"Well, why wouldn't it look like this?" I asked him.

"I guess I never thought about blacks celebrating Christmas just like we do. Have you ever seen a card like this?" he wanted to know. I admitted that I had not. "I wonder where they found it." We both looked at the card as if it had arrived from outer space.

I remember that as a child I had been bewildered by separate restrooms and drinking fountains for blacks and whites. During a trip to Fort Worth, I couldn't comprehend why I wasn't allowed to drink from a fountain in Woolworth's department store. My mother grabbed my arm and exclaimed, "Jerry, you can't drink from that water! See the sign? It says 'colored.'"

"Mom, the water looks clear to me," I said.

"Jerry, white people have their own toilets and water," she said.

"Why?" I asked.

"Because," was all she said.

By the time the Stars played our first game in May 1960, our country had witnessed several impressive events. In February four black students from North Carolina Agricultural and Technical College demanded lunch at Woolworth's in Greensboro and were refused service, starting other nonviolent racial protests in the South. By August the same four students were finally served their lunches. In March the military announced that 3,500 American troops were being sent to Vietnam, and the U.S. Senate passed the Civil Rights Bill on April 8. These events took place miles away from Jacksboro, but I knew they were important.

Before the start of the first Stars game of the 1960 season, I learned that tragedy struck our team on the day I had returned to Tech. After I left the Graham Field following the final game of the 1959 season. Mr. Sedberry and four of my teammates—Alfred Ray, T. J. Hawkins, Emmitt Johnson, and Hubert "Bo" Beasley—left Mr. Sedberry's Café and drove to Possum Kingdom Lake in T. J.'s car.

They ran off old Bunger Road on the way to the lake and hit a large post oak tree. Alfred was thrown through the windshield. He was paralyzed and died in Graham Hospital a few days later.

I subscribed to our hometown newspapers while I was away at Tech so that I could read about the events in Jacksboro. I missed news of Alfred's death because back then black people weren't allowed to place obituaries in the white newspapers. If I had known about his death, I would have attended Alfred Ray's funeral.

After our starting catcher was gone, the Stars were not the same. I recall fewer games from our second season than I do from our first. The first season was bright with new experiences for me, but memories from the second are dimmer because I knew we weren't as good a team.

I knew our time was short and our light was fading, but we had a large, happy crowd on that first Sunday afternoon at Spudder Park in late May 1960. As the pregame ceremonies were about to start, Mr. Sedberry gently patted me on the back and told me that Emmitt would take Alfred's place as catcher. I grasped his hand and told him I was very sorry about Alfred.

Although Mr. Sedberry and I were sharing a quiet moment in memory of Alfred, the fans surrounding us were boisterous. They were amazed to see us resplendent in brand-new uniforms. We had also been individually fitted for our cap size. Even our blue stockings were new.

Our uniforms were light gray with navy-blue pin stripes and navy-blue cording around the neck and down the front, where five blue buttons shone brightly in the sun. The word "Stars" in navy blue ran across the chest. Mine had the number 6 on the left sleeve. My back read "Faith Cleaners" from Wichita Falls, its motto "The City that Faith Built." The pants were short knickers style with a four-button fly and matching navy-blue stockings. No Texans were ever prouder of their uniforms than my teammates and I were on that day.

Mr. Sedberry found a recording of the National Anthem to open the game. I stood by my teammates and proudly listened to the music of our country. We were all citizens of the United States as we listened to the same anthem, watched the same flag, and wore matching uniforms for the first time. Most teams and fans would take this scene for granted at the start of every game, but for us it was a special day.

After the National Anthem, the speaker system blared "Sweet Georgia Brown," and my teammates laughed and showed off during our warm-ups. They tossed baseballs from behind their backs, rolled them down their arms to their hands, and caught them with their caps, all the while doing neat little dance steps, similar to line dancing. They would sometimes stand along the infield foul line and dance together to the music. Fat led the choreography, but T. J., "Puddin," and Bo could boogie too.

Mr. Sedberry was pleased with himself and the festive arrangements. He laughed a lot and said, "Everything is fine in the summertime!"

I appreciated his enthusiasm, but my mood darkened when I learned who Mr. Sedberry had chosen for us to face on opening day. A brand-new semi-pro team from Bowie, Texas, had just arrived at the field. The Jackrabbits were an all-white team because everyone in Bowie was white. I was worried that Mr. Sedberry's choice of opponent would be hostile toward us when our pregame celebration ended and the game began.

I was on the mound, and Emmitt Johnson was now my catcher, replacing Alfred as best he could. The Jackrabbits were not a good ball club, and we started beating them badly.

Around the bottom of the eighth inning, Bobby Herron showed up. He had been working late. Bobby eyed the score and the new opposition and said, "Where are these guys from?"

"Bowie," Fat said.

If a black person could turn white, Bobby came close to it. With a pale, scared glance at Mr. Sedberry, he said, "Carl, are we going to play them at their home field?"

"Yes, we play them in Bowie next Sunday afternoon," he replied. "Why do you want to know?"

"Boys, I'm afraid to go to Bowie," Bobby told us.

"I am afraid to go to Bowie too," Rabbit said. "I remember the first time I went from Wichita Falls to Dallas. I went through Bowie, and I saw a black man hung from a tree by his neck."

They were terrified. When we took the field again, I'd never seen us make so many errors. If we hadn't already built up such a sizable lead, I'm sure we would have lost that game. We finally got out of the inning, but just as Casey and all his fans felt in the poem "Casey at the Bat," there was no joy in Wichita Falls. Our team reluctantly agreed to meet the next Sunday in Bowie, but I really doubted we would play.

To my surprise, the Stars drove in from Wichita Falls for the game in Bowie, and I came by myself from Jacksboro to meet them. Every single one of the Stars came ready to play although they were scared to death.

After our warm-ups, my teammates ducked their heads and tried to disappear into the dugout. I told them, "You always tell me not to worry and that you'll take care of me. I pledge to take care of you today."

"Jerry, there's only one of you," Rabbit reminded me, glancing quickly at the large, all-white crowd.

I looked around and feared for the worst. Although the entire Bowie police force and the Montague County sheriff's department were present, I did not want to take my chances on their protecting me. Our adrenaline must have been at an all-time high because Rabbit and Bobby hit their first two pitches so far over the fence that no one ever found the balls.

A few innings later, I gave up back-to-back home runs, the only game in which I ever did that. However, I overcame that setback to pitch well that day, and we whipped them badly. When the last out was called, the Stars jumped in their cars and raced out of Bowie.

The game in Bowie put our team under great psychological stress, and several of our regular players stopped attending the next few games. We were in danger of not having enough players to field a team for the popular Juneteenth tournament, which surprised me because my teammates really looked forward to that tournament and celebration.

We participated in one weekend tournament a year, the

annual Juneteenth Tournament in Ranger, Texas. Juneteenth commemorates June 19, 1865, the date that U.S. General Gordon Granger read the Emancipation Proclamation announcing the end of slavery in Galveston. Juneteenth was a huge celebration in Texas in the late 1950s and early 1960s, and the Stars enjoyed the holiday by playing other black teams in the Ranger tournament.

The fans were, in fact, the best part of the tournament. All of the Stars fans plus fans of teams from all over Texas traveled to those games. Fat told me he had never seen so many black people in a white town at one time.

Early in 1960 Mr. Sedberry scouted a few new players because he wanted to win the tournament. He discovered that the talented black players in the area already played for other teams. When I heard his unsuccessful scouting report, I had an idea.

"I have a couple of friends in Jacksboro who might like to play for the Stars. Of course, they're both white," I said.

He stopped what he was doing and looked me in the eye. Finally he said, "Let me talk to the team."

Mr. Sedberry motioned for the Stars to stop loading their cars and join us. Then he turned to the team and said, "Jerry wants to bring a couple of his white friends along to play next time. What do you think of that?"

"If Jerry recommends them and they're anything like him, let them play," Rabbit said. Everyone nodded. The Stars wouldn't have cared if my friends were purple if they could play baseball.

Later that week I spoke to Monroe Henderson and Tony Clark. They already knew about my playing with a black team, but they had not considered playing with the Stars until I extended the invitation and told them the team would be happy to have them.

Monroe and Tony loved playing baseball and readily agreed to play for the Stars, but they wouldn't be able to join us until the championship game on Sunday at the Juneteenth tournament. Monroe was especially eager to join the team. He enjoyed every team he ever played with.

When the Stars finally arrived late Friday evening in Ranger, we watched the end of the games the local teams were playing. We never had enough fields for everyone to play during the day, so the teams played all night Friday and into Saturday on one field. I had learned about the all-night games our first year in Ranger, making a fool out of myself in the process.

In 1959 when I had asked what motel we'd use in Ranger, my teammates laughed at me. Bobby said, "White boy, there's no place blacks can stay in Ranger." I hadn't thought of that and looked sheepishly at my bag of clean underwear, socks, jersey, and toiletries.

Bobby added, "We sleep in our cars, but we don't expect you to do that."

Then I told them I'd sleep in my car too. They stared at me in disbelief for a moment. Then they looked at each other and grinned. I undressed to my T-shirt and shorts, wadded up my uniform for a pillow, and stuck my feet out of the passenger window so that I could sleep in my back seat.

Mr. Sedberry quietly approached the car and said, "Mr. Craft, you don't have to do this."

"Yes, I do," I said.

A few minutes later, Rabbit brought me a spare pillow and some mosquito spray. He hesitated, then added, "Good night. You're a good man."

The next morning, I gathered up some money and drove to Ranger to buy us hamburgers and chips. We already had sodas iced down, but I bought the food because Ranger and its restaurants were segregated.

By the second tournament, I was prepared to camp. I'd packed plenty of pillows, blankets, and mosquito spray. I was more comfortable, but we didn't sleep much because we were having such a good time.

I pitched Friday night's game against Hamlin, which we won. We socialized all night Friday and into Saturday morning, visiting with one another and the other teams and spectators in the stands. A team that lost early stayed for the fun. Everyone had to stay near the baseball fields because they couldn't go into Ranger. The crowded conditions made the tournament a little rowdy at times, but most of us enjoyed meeting new people and talking to them.

We were a bit dirty and smelly by game time on Saturday. Fat pitched, and we won, qualifying us for the Sunday afternoon championship game against San Augustine, a small town in East Texas next to the Louisiana border. Monroe and Tony arrived in time for the game, and Monroe started at third base. Tony played right field, and I pitched, winning 5–3.

When Monroe and Tony joined us for the championship game, we shifted Vernon "Puddin" Higgins from third to second so that Monroe could play third base. Monroe was the best ballplayer of my era from Jacksboro. He was a superior infielder with a strong throwing arm.

Tony, on the other hand, was not a great athlete, but he was a good outfielder and could play second base for us in a pinch. He was a couple of years younger than Monroe and was simply pleased to be offered the chance to play baseball with us.

The Stars had become very comfortable playing with me, but with two more white players on the team, I believe my teammates were a little uneasy. They were all kinder and more considerate with three white guys around.

Monroe does not remember any resentment from the Stars when he and Tony joined the team for the tournament. He thinks if they felt any, they disguised it. They were happy to have help for the tournament.

After the final game, Tony, Monroe, and I caravanned to a barbeque dinner at the all-white Ranger Country Club, which the teams had somehow rented. I don't know how they arranged it or what it cost, but we were all there. In 1960 Ranger was home to some very affluent families, a fine country club, and a nice golf course.

Tony later told me that as he stood in the crowd at the country club, he felt for the first time in his life what it might be like to be in a minority. "I feel welcome, but I don't feel like I belong," he told me shortly before he and Monroe left.

"It's OK," I told him. "Please stay. You helped us win today, so you are a part of us."

"No, we're calling it an evening," he said. "I believe I've learned a lot in a few hours about a whole group of people I've lived beside all my life but have never known." They thanked me as we said our goodbyes.

Before the Stars could eat and socialize, we needed a

good shower. We were lucky enough to enjoy the hot showers, soap, and clean towels at the country club. Showers were a wonderful luxury for us that teams today take for granted. That was our first shower as a team in nearly two years.

The large, open shower room had about ten showerheads. Both teams from the championship game had a long, hot shower, and we popped each other with towels and sang songs.

We hated dressing in our sweaty uniforms after showering, but we had no extra clothes. As we emerged from the locker rooms, a wonderful smell surrounded our slightly stale one. Designated chefs had been at their trade all day, cooking barbeque. Slow cookers lined the room, full of chicken, brisket, and ribs for the nearly three hundred players, family, and friends who were enjoying full access to the country club.

When June 19 rolls around each year, I always think of the two wonderful weekends I spent celebrating Juneteenth with my friends.

Chapter Eight
Lessons from a Black Man

After the excitement of the Juneteenth tournament, Mr. Sedberry wanted to keep us busy. He felt that our season had taken a turn for the better and was thrilled when the Trojans invited us to play on the Fourth of July at Windthorst. We had played against the Trojans at the Graham field on the Fourth of July during the previous season. That 1959 Independence Day game had been such a success that their team returned the favor by asking us to bring our families to Windthorst.

This Fourth of July they had a new baseball field, a tremendous improvement from the pasture we had played on the year before. A large crowd, half black people and half white, sat in the July sun, enjoying the game and each other. Although the Stars, Trojans, and their fans got along, they did not sit together. The stands appeared to be segregated because the white fans got to the game first, and they sat wherever they liked. That's where the rest of the white fans joined them. I don't think they were necessarily segregating themselves by race, just by the team they supported.

Behind home plate a five-foot gap divided the blacks and

whites. I suppose that they could have chosen to sit closer together, but that just wasn't done back then. Our fans sat together to support our team, and our fans happened to be black.

Of all the white teams we played against, we were most comfortable facing Windthorst. About an hour into the game, the Windthorst dairy farmers again began making their temporary substitutions. It was milking time. I was still amused by the fact that we allowed them to go milk their cows in the middle of a baseball game, but I wasn't a dairy farmer. I was a rancher, and ranchers don't milk. Certain times of the year are busier for us than others, but we don't have the daily commitment to milking that dairy farmers do. As I watched them leave for their farms, I was grateful I was a rancher.

Even without the dairy farmers participating, the game was a close one. In the top of the ninth, Wayne Fisher was on second and I was on first. Rabbit slammed a high, outside fastball off the fence in right center. Fisher rounded third and headed for home. I was not far behind him. Mr. Sedberry waved both of us in.

"Run, Fisher! Run!" I hollered behind him.

The Windthorst catcher Schreiber had his mask off and was crouched on the third base side of home plate, waiting for the throw, his huge left leg angled to protect the plate. Fisher made a beautiful hook slide with his right leg toward the front of the plate. Schreiber caught the throw and dove for Fisher, but the tag was too late.

I heard the umpire call "Safe!" and signal as I slid head-first to the backside of the plate, my left hand extended.

"Safe! Safe! They're both safe!" the umpire screamed.

We were all stunned about what had just happened. The crowd seemed equally stunned. Then all the fans, both black and white, stood up and clapped. One of the unique things about the game of baseball is that average players can sometimes achieve greatness in the face of adversity, and average fans can appreciate a great play. At those times, both players and fans are color blind.

We all talked about the play a great deal as we celebrated the Fourth after the game, final score Stars 5, Trojans 4. We had played very good baseball in Windthorst, against a solid ball club. When all of our players were present, we could beat anyone.

The town was incredibly supportive of the game, turning out to see us play and to eat with us afterward. A couple of tables full of food were set up by the slow cookers, holding piles of German sausage. We passed down the line of tables, holding our paper plates, and the cooks would serve us the sausage.

After we filled our plates, everyone sat in the bleachers and ate. Although the game was over, we still sat separately in the stands. The children cheered the fireworks display, watching as the adults set off bottle rockets, cherry bombs, sparklers, and roman candles.

Our spirits had been lifted during the Fourth of July holiday game in Windthorst, so Mr. Sedberry decided to schedule a rare double-header in distant Oklahoma City. He claimed he couldn't get anyone else to play that weekend and that the Braves wanted a double-header. If we were to travel all the way to Oklahoma, we might as well play two games.

Monroe made the Oklahoma City trip, and we rode there

together in my car. "Mo" didn't care where we were playing. He simply loved playing and was happy to help the Stars again after his enjoyable experience at the Ranger tournament. He agreed, though, that the time and distance involved in playing a double-header in Oklahoma City meant a long day. Monroe's natural position was shortstop, but he could play third base just as well. I told him we would probably need him at third in Oklahoma because Fat was firmly entrenched at short.

Sam and T. J. were supposed to pitch the first game for us, but they didn't show up, so I got an unexpected start for game one of the double-header. I had planned on pitching that day, but the idea of pitching two games did not appeal to me. I hoped the other pitchers would arrive soon.

The Braves had some great players, and we struggled to win 2–1. When our other two pitchers still had not appeared, Mr. Sedberry tried to get Fat to pitch the second game. He refused. Mr. Sedberry looked around for another pitcher, and his eye fell on Monroe.

"Mr. Craft, does your friend pitch?" he asked me.

"Yes, but he doesn't enjoy pitching as much as he does playing infield. Why don't you let me start, and let's hope relief shows up soon," I told him.

"Are you sure, Mr. Craft?" he asked.

"I'll go as far as I can, Mr. Sedberry," I told him. "Maybe someone will show up after we get the second game started." Both of us doubted this because it was already late afternoon.

When I finally signaled Mr. Sedberry to the mound two hours later, I was struggling. We were seven innings into the second game and trailing 1–2. He motioned toward Fat and Monroe, and they joined us on the mound.

"Fat, I need you to pitch the rest of the game. We'll move Monroe to shortstop. Mr. Craft can take third base," Mr. Sedberry told them.

Fat flatly refused. He crossed his arms, stuck his nose in the air, and told us he would not do it.

Fat considered himself the reigning king at shortstop, and I believe he probably feared a person of Monroe's talent might threaten his throne. Fat was a very good pitcher, and in other circumstances he would have grudgingly agreed to relieve me in a second game of a double-header, but with Monroe there, the situation was very different.

I looked around, not knowing what to do. "I have nothing left," I told the men on the mound. "Someone is going to have to pitch." I staggered wearily off the mound and toward third base. A smattering of applause followed me.

"I'll do it," Monroe volunteered. That was how Monroe became the Stars' second white pitcher for one game.

Monroe remembers pitching for the Stars, not because he was that good at it, but there was no other option. Monroe held his own that day by preventing the Braves from scoring, but we could not put any players across the plate, losing the game 1–2. So this unusual situation meant that I was both the winning and the losing pitcher on the same day, and I pitched sixteen full innings.

Late in July we played the Sheppard Air Force team at their base in Wichita Falls. Their personnel changed with every game as troops were deployed, but their teams were always all white. They did not have a separate black ball club like Fort Wolters did.

Sheppard's baseball team never attracted large crowds. Airmen who might have the day off preferred to do other things with their Sundays than watch baseball. Our fans were welcome at the games, but sometimes the A.P.s, "Air Police"—the equivalent of the army's M.P.s—would question our fans as they tried to enter the base.

With the Civil Rights Movement beginning, security was getting tighter at the military bases than Mr. Sedberry had ever seen. When our team arrived at the gate, we were wearing our uniforms, but the A.P.s asked us for our drivers' licenses and recorded the numbers. The A.P.s then gave us directions to the field, pointed toward the ballpark, and waved us in.

When a large caravan of our fans showed up, the A.P.s were not as receptive. A new shift of A.P.s had started and had no idea a black baseball team was playing that day. Several cars full of black people arriving simultaneously made them nervous, and after much explanation and a few phone calls, the fans were allowed inside.

Our fans were not pleased that they had been delayed, but they had spent all of their lives being treated as second-class citizens. They did not waste a lot of time complaining about it or resenting their treatment. They had, in many ways, come to expect it.

Once the fans arrived at the baseball field, they were disappointed by its appearance. Home plate faced toward the north, and the outfield fences were wire. At least there were lights, so they knew they would see the end of the game. The stands also held fewer white fans than at other "white" fields, which meant our fans had greater freedom in selecting where they wanted to sit.

The weeks that followed involved several losses that I'd prefer not to recall because I didn't enjoy losing, but one game was memorable because I received a standing ovation, my first ever. We were on the road for a game against the Pied Pipers, an all-black team from Hamlin, which is northwest of Abilene and over two hours away from Wichita Falls. We played Hamlin on their high school's diamond, which featured below-ground dugouts topped by concrete roofs. For Hamlin's game against the Stars, a large, all-black crowd filled the stands, about half of them from Graham and Wichita Falls.

I threw a dropping curve to the lead-off batter, and he popped it up about halfway down the third base line, too far for the catcher or third baseman to field, but just across from my position as pitcher. As I sprinted toward the weak pop-up and dove for the foul ball, I miraculously caught it and slid into the Hamlin dugout. In the confusion, I briefly lost the ball but caught it on my chest with my glove and bare right hand.

The Hamlin players also caught me during my unexpected journey into their dugout. I lay across a row of players as the umpire ran over and descended into the dugout to ask, "Well, did he catch it?"

"He did," one of the Hamlin players said, "and it was some catch!"

The umpire called the out while the Hamlin players dusted me off. I emerged from the dugout with the ball, and our fans rose to their feet in applause. I was startled by the standing ovation and stood there for a moment not knowing how to react.

I thought I should do something, so I took off my cap and waved it toward them. When I did that, the Hamlin side also rose and applauded. I then realized to that baseball crowd it didn't make any difference what color I was. If a player made a great play, they appreciated and applauded it.

We easily defeated the Pied Pipers, and as we gathered in the parking lot for some tailgating, the Hamlin manager came over and shook my hand. All of us were visiting, and the manager asked me, "What's your name, white boy?"

I told him my name and where I was from.

"You're OK," he told me. He then told me that after I had made my catch in his team's dugout and was walking back to the mound, he told his team, "We're going to have our hands full with that white boy today."

"How do you know that?" one of his players had asked.

"A pitcher who will go to the lengths he did just to catch a foul ball will also find a way to beat you. That white boy is a winner!"

At the end of July, we were scheduled to play against an all-black team from Stamford, an old cowboy town about two-and-a-half hours west of Jacksboro. The Stamford baseball field was part of the town's rodeo arena. Both football and baseball games were held there, with the baseball diamond positioned at an angle in the elongated arena. Those were tough games because we played on dirt.

The Bulldogs didn't have much on the field that day. I don't recall many of the details of our game against them, but as I was sitting next to Mr. Sedberry on the bench, I casually commented to him that their pitcher wasn't any good. I thought about this for a few minutes and then asked him, "Why do we see so few good black pitchers?"

Mr. Sedberry suddenly became more talkative that half

inning than he had been all day, and his words have remained with me over the years.

"I don't know," he responded. "That's why we have you."

"I appreciate that, but really, we have other athletes on our team who have the talent to play anywhere on the field, like Fat, Rabbit, and Bobby."

"Well, I believe our team lacks discipline, and pitchers need a lot of discipline," he said.

He told me, "Mr. Craft, your teammates want to hit home runs. You, on the other hand, have more discipline in your right arm than my entire team does. Does that mean we want to play on white teams? No, we don't."

"Whoa, Mr. Sedberry. I'm not just a white player. We're a team, and we're playing together," I said.

"I guess so, Mr. Craft. But I would hate to lose our kind of game. You see, integration scares me. On the one hand, I certainly want years of injustice righted. On the other hand, though, I'm frightened my team and even our whole race will lose its identity. And what about fun? Do you think that any of us would have this much fun if one of us were playing on an all-white team?"

We were silent through the rest of the game and left the tailgating early together. He said nothing for a long time in the car.

"I hope I didn't offend you," he finally said.

"No, you didn't. But I was wondering what brought all this up?" I asked.

He grinned and slapped me on the back. "I thought about our wonderful two Fourth of July celebrations with our Windthorst friends and about black and white children playing together. I thought especially about how both teams appreciated how well we all played baseball together as athletes and men."

Underneath his optimism, I knew from previous conversations with Mr. Sedberry that he revered the Negro Leagues and was grieving their demise. I saw how hurt he was that the leagues he treasured would soon be gone forever. Mr. Sedberry recognized that there would be a price to pay for the integration of Major League Baseball, but how could a player or fan truly be compensated for the loss of an entire league and its teams?

He had seen the black owners of the Negro League teams fight failing attendance, struggle to make payrolls, and sell off their stars to survive. The end was inevitable. The glory days of Mr. Sedberry's beloved black baseball were gone. As we traveled together, I became curious about one aspect of integration that I had never asked Mr. Sedberry about.

"How are the black players ever going to become major leaguers and prove that they are athletes equal to or better than white players?" I asked him.

"White boy, they already are," he replied rather testily.

"You, as a black man, believe that, but the white man sure doesn't," I said.

"Why would I care what they believe anyway? If I believe what some of them do—that I'm not any better than a farm animal—then how could a farm animal possibly play such a beautiful game so well?"

CHAPTER NINE
THE LAST INNING

T exas in July can be a cruel place, the sun and heat bearing down on baseball teams, grass, and livestock. July 1960 was especially difficult for me and the Stars, but the reason we struggled had nothing to do with the weather. When Mr. Sedberry made his weekly call to me to let me know when, where, and what time we were playing, I received a terrible shock. His voice wavered over the phone line as he asked if Monroe and Tony would try to be there. I told him I didn't know. Then he hesitated and added, "If you know of a white catcher, we could sure use one."

"Why?" I asked.

"You see, Emmitt was killed this week in a car wreck," he said.

I suddenly realized we had lost two catchers in two years to car accidents. I knew instantly that the fate of the Stars was sealed. I don't recall the team we played on Sunday, but I do remember that we lost badly.

When I first arrived at the field, Rabbit took me aside.

"Did you know Emmitt was killed in a car wreck in East Texas?" he asked. Our eyes met.

"Yes. Mr. Sedberry told me over the phone," I said. "Why didn't you call me to let me know when the funeral was?"

He shrugged his shoulders.

"Did you attend it?" I asked.

"Sure."

"This is going to be the end of the Stars," I told him.

"Yeah, we lost a really good catcher back when Alfred died. Emmitt wasn't as good, but he was dependable. Mr. Sedberry's been shaking the bushes to find us another good catcher," Rabbit said.

I glanced at home plate to see that our starting catcher was none other than old "Toothless" Tommy Jones, the same catcher who two years before had complained to Mr. Sedberry when my curveball damaged his baseball-weary knees. Tommy had not played catcher in over a year, and his baseball skills had certainly not improved during his time off.

"I guess Mr. Sedberry hasn't been shaking the bushes hard enough," I told Rabbit as I headed for the bullpen.

The team rapidly fell apart. In addition to catching, Emmitt had served as team co-captain with Rabbit. After church on Sunday Emmitt and Rabbit had rounded up all our ballplayers for the games. Together, they knew everyone's habits and hideouts. Without their motivating us, the wonderful world of Stars baseball was no longer fun.

We had so few players participating that for several games late in our last summer together we would drag fans out of the stands to join us. They looked ridiculous in their thin slacks and shirts. Any hope of recruiting additional players, white or black, was next to impossible that late in the season. Good players were already playing for other teams and could not be convinced to join a losing one. With our losing record, team morale sank.

We were just a shell of the great club we once were. Mr. Sedberry continued to try, but he could not recruit anyone. Even black teenagers were not tempted. They had begged us to give them a chance in 1959 when we were winning and had good players. Everyone wanted a chance to play with the Stars, but not now. The once-mighty Stars were fading.

I was becoming very unhappy with our team, and Mr. Sedberry knew it. He made me promises that we would improve. Our next game was against Anna at Trinity Park in Fort Worth.

Before the game, Mr. Sedberry told me, "One of the best black outfielders I've seen in some time is going to join us. He catches balls with a basket catch, just like Willie Mays."

Catching a ball at waist level didn't seem like such a good idea to me, but we really needed some help. Tony and Monroe had already given up on us. I was close to quitting too, so I told Mr. Sedberry that I really hoped the new player would help us.

Anna had a good, all-black ball club, and when they got on base, they quickly learned they could steal every base off old Tommy, the toothless catcher. In the fifth inning, I had struck out six batters, but the bases were loaded because Tommy was dropping the third strike. He seemed worn out. Mr. Sedberry called time and came to the mound to tell me the good news.

"Mr. Craft," he said. "That great outfielder I was telling you about is here. I'm going to put him in left field."

"I wish he was a catcher," I said.

The young man dashed onto the field. He wore a bright red uniform with "Red Devils" across the back of his jersey. He was extremely excited and rushed to the mound to introduce himself as the next Willie Mays.

"All you have to do to win this game is let Anna hit everything to me," he said.

I wasn't one for showboat moves like basket catches. The real Willie Mays had made them his trademark. His coaches had long ago quit asking him to stop catching balls in such a risky fashion, but the fans had come to love and expect the spectacular catches.

As fate and the gods of baseball decreed, the next Anna batter lofted my curveball to "Willie Jr." He hovered under the ball and pounded his glove, shouting, "It's mine! It's mine!"

Holding his glove and right hand at his waist, he prepared to show us his stuff. The baseball hit him squarely on top of his head. It didn't carom off at an angle but bounced twenty feet straight up in the air. America's future superstar lay spread-eagled and unconscious as four runners laughingly circled the bases and scored.

I watched as our players tried to revive the new left fielder, and then I turned and walked to our dugout. Curiously, I didn't think my baseball career would end like this, during an uneventful regular-season game. Like most athletes, I had envisioned a no-hitter or a championship game as my last time on the field.

I thought about what I would do next. My life without the Stars flashed briefly through my mind. I would probably go back to full-time ranching. We had only played games on Wednesday nights in Graham and Sunday afternoons in

Spudder Park in Wichita Falls or on the road, so I had continued to work on the ranch the entire time I played for the Stars.

I knew I would never see them play again. I had no desire to watch their continued demise. I disliked participating in the team's downfall, and I didn't want to watch them from the stands.

I picked up my warm-up jacket and extended my hand to Mr. Sedberry. He shook it, and I gave him a hug.

"Mr. Sedberry, it's been a real ride, but this is it," I said.

"No, just give us one more chance, Mr. Craft," he said.

"I can't do that. It's not fun anymore," I told him. I told everyone goodbye. In July 1960, I walked away from the Stars and baseball forever.

Mr. Sedberry remained the team's coach. He later told me, "When you quit, that was the end of the Stars. I knew I would never have another team like them, but I wanted to continue coaching. There was never another team like the Stars. That kind of team, if you are lucky, only happens once in a lifetime. I was lucky."

The Stars folded three years after my departure, ending ten years of local all-black league baseball in Wichita Falls and Graham. Mr. Sedberry fought to keep the tradition alive by forming an independent team of young black players called the Graham Junkyard Dogs in 1963. He recruited teenagers from Graham for his new team because they were more available for games and were more consistent in their attendance at games and practices than the Stars had been. The teenagers really wanted to play ball, and Mr. Sedberry could count on them to show up for games.

Mr. Sedberry thoroughly enjoyed baseball, and instead of being discouraged by the disappearance of the Stars, he introduced the game to the next generation of players. He later told me the Junkyard Dogs didn't possess the same talent and didn't win as many games as the Stars had, but being their coach was very rewarding. They wanted to learn and were very serious about playing baseball. Mr. Sedberry gave the gift of baseball to the young people in his community, and I will always be grateful to him for giving the gift of the Stars to me.

AFTERWORD

I never thought my experiences with the Stars were news-worthy until 1993, when Hollace Weiner of the *Fort Worth Star-Telegram* called me to ask about my involvement in the West Texas Colored League.

"Did this all truly happen?" she asked me.

"Yes," I told her. "It did, but no one has ever been inter-ested in it."

Hollace had been covering a story on my sister, and Lin-da had told her, "If you want a really good story, talk to my brother."

I spoke with Hollace a few times on the phone, but I was too busy to give her a formal interview. Then a few days later a photographer for the *Star-Telegram* walked into my office unannounced. Hollace joined him and said, "If you want to throw me out of your office, you certainly can, but I just have to do this story."

I laughed and said, "If you are that passionate about this story, let's do it."

Her story awoke memories that I had long forgotten. I started to wonder where my former teammates were. We had gone our separate ways. After the *Star-Telegram* interview, I started trying to find my old teammates. I found Mr. Sedberry first, right where he had always been, on Lincoln Street in Graham.

He, Rabbit, and I had lunch, and he tried to recall where the other players were. We were helped by Channel 8, the local ABC-TV affiliate, and its sport editor, John Pronk, who found Bobby Lee Herron and Clarence "Rabbit" Myles. John asked them to come to Jacksboro, and he produced a documentary on our team's playing days.

Rabbit had remained in touch with some of the guys. Rabbit asked Earnest "Fat" Locke to breakfast, and we met him in Wichita Falls. We began to meet regularly and compare memories. I was sad to hear that many of our teammates had already died. Today, only Monroe, Rabbit, and I are left.

During our breakfast meetings, Rabbit, Fat, and I discussed all the changes we'd seen in baseball. We lamented the loss of town teams and semi-pro baseball that had been a way of life for seventy-five years in the small towns around Graham and Jacksboro. Those games had been the one thing to do on the weekends.

On February 20, 1999, the Southwestern Bell Telephone Company sponsored the African American History Month Family Day and Negro League Baseball Reunion (Southwest) at the African American Museum at Fair Park in Dallas. Mr. Sedberry, Fat, Rabbit, and I were invited to participate in the activities.

After a few speeches, thirteen former baseball players, including me, participated in a roundtable discussion, led by Larry Lester. Larry is the director of the Negro Baseball League Museum in Kansas City, Missouri, and a voting member of the National Baseball Hall of Fame. The very first question from the audience to me was "What are you doing here?"

There were a few chuckles from the crowd, and then I told my story. Some of the players around me spoke eloquently about their experiences. Rabbit and Mr. Sedberry, seated on either side of me, leaned in to whisper, "We're scared to death." Neither enjoyed public speaking.

After the roundtable discussion, we were directed to the museum's large rotunda, where long tables were stacked with crates of baseballs. The outside doors opened and in tumbled hundreds of children.

I had never autographed a baseball before. To my surprise, I discovered it's not easy to do. Because a ball is round, not flat, it's hard to hold with your left hand and sign with your right. We signed hundreds of baseballs, and when we ran out of baseballs, we signed their T-shirts, caps, or whatever scraps of paper they had with them.

After the last of the children ran happily out the door with their pieces of history, we were tired. We agreed it was one of the most rewarding days of our lives as we traveled back to Jacksboro. We also laughed that all of our autographs would be worn off that weekend as the balls would be put into play in sandlots all over Dallas. I think that's a much better use of them than their gathering dust on a shelf.

I've always loved children, and in a flash my own children, Jay, Sue, and Clint, have grown up. They had fun and played the games they loved. Baseball shaped my outlook on life, and I believe that as a parent and grandparent my greatest reward is watching my children and their children be happy. I hope that others will learn a little bit about baseball and a little bit about life from my story.

References

Craft, Jerry. 1999. Unpublished interview by Mary Nell Westbrook. Jacksboro, Texas. January 24.

Daily Toreador. 1956. "Extra! Finally! Tech Makes SWC, Tech Breaks SWC Jinx." May 12.

Henderson, Monroe. 2007. Interview by Kathleen Sullivan. Fort Worth, Texas. July 31.

Horton, Thomas F. 1975. *The History of Jack County.* Fort Worth: J. Robert Dennis.

Huckaby, Ida Laster. 1949. *Ninety-Four Years in Jack County: 1854–1948.* Austin: Steck.

Jack County Genealogical Society. 1985. *The History of Jack County.* Dallas: Curtis Media Corp.

Myles, Clarence "Rabbit." 2007. Interview by Kathleen Sullivan. Wichita Falls, Texas. February 17.

Peterson, Robert. 1970. *Only the Ball Was White: A History of Legendary Black Players and All-Black Professional Teams.* New York: Gramercy Books.

Rampersad, Arnold. 1997. *Jackie Robinson: A Biography.* New York: Ballantine.

Sedberry, Carl. 1999. Unpublished interview by Mary Nell Westbrook. Graham, Texas. March 3.

Acknowledgments

Many thanks to Texas Tech University Press, especially Judith Keeling, for their continued support of our work. We also appreciate copyeditor Karen Medlin's terrific suggestions during this second half of our "double header." Finally, we applaud our home teams, including Pamela Craft, Johnny Stephens, and Connor Porter, who have cheered us through our second book. We love you all.

INDEX

The bolded locator **P** refers to the photograph section; the number following is the photograph number.

major-league baseball, 56–57
Massengale, Jess, **P 2**
Massengale. Don, **P 3**
McConnell, Eddie, 19
Midway Falcons, 25, 32
Murray, Bobby, 19, 26
    Jacksboro High School football team and, **P 5**
Myers, Shine, **P 2**
Myers, Wallace "Hogcaller," 23, **P 2**
Myles, Arnita Campbell, **P 13**
Myles, Clarence, Jr., **P 12**
Myles, Clarence "Rabbit," xii, 36–37, 43–44, 45, 53, 54, 72, 80, 89–90, 96,
    P 1, **P 13**, **P 14**
    as basketball coach, **P 14**
Myles, Melvin, **P 14**

Negro Leagues, 40, 88
Noel, Bert, **P 2**

Oklahoma City Braves double-header, 81–83
Oil Belt League, 5, 33

Parks, Rosa, xii
Patoosis, Pat, **P 2**
Patton, Keith, **P 3**
Pearson, Jerry, **P 9**
Phelps, Dick, **P 9**
Phillips, Warner, **P 9**
Pronk, John, 46, 96

Randolph, Masters, **P 2**
Ranger, Texas, xiii
    Country Club, 77
    tournament in, xiii, 73–78
Ray, Alfred, 8, 12, 13, 36, 70
Richardson, Gordon, **P 9**
Rickey, Branch, 40

ABOUT THE AUTHORS

Jerry Craft is a rancher and former mayor of Jacksboro, Texas, his hometown.

Kathleen Sullivan has taught at Southern Methodist University and the University of Texas at Arlington. She lives in Arlington, Texas.